Tao of the Ride

Motorcycles and the Mechanics of the Soul

Garri Garripoli
and Friends

Health Communications, Inc.
Deerfield Beach, Florida

www.hci-online.com

We would like to acknowledge the following publishers and individuals for permission to reprint the following material.

Grateful Dead lyrics (used as epigraphs at the beginning of each chapter) by Robert Hunter, copyright Ice Nine Publishing Company, Inc. Used by permission.

"What a long strange trip it's been," (lyric used in running text) by Robert Hunter, copyright Ice Nine Publishing Company, Inc. Used by permission.

Material contributed by Dr. Martin Jack Rosenblum, including "Secret Lingo," reprinted by permission of Dr. Martin Jack Rosenblum. ©1998 Dr. Martin Jack Rosenblum.

Material contributed by James M. Garripoli reprinted by permission of James M. Garripoli. ©1999 James M. Garripoli.

Material contributed by Wai "Franki" Yang reprinted by permission of Wai "Franki" Yang. ©1999 Wai "Franki" Yang.

(continued on page 141)

Library of Congress Cataloging-in-Publication Data

Garripoli, Garri, date.
  Tao of the ride: motocycles and the mechanics of the soul / Garri Garripoli and friends.
    p. cm.
   ISBN 1-55874-670-6 (trade paper)
   1. Life. 2. Philosophy, Taoist I. Title
  BD431.G24 1999
  128—dc21   98-24251
                                                       CIP

©1999 Garri Garripoli
ISBN 1-55874-670-6

Publisher: Health Communications, Inc.
              3201 S.W. 15th Street
              Deerfield Beach, FL 33442-8190

Cover design and photography by Garri Garripoli
Layout by Lisa Camp

I dedicate this book to my wife Daisy Lee
who has supported me in the infinite ways a true friend,
riding partner and lover can.
This is also to all the wives, husbands and partners
who support their riding companions and
understand in their hearts
what the Ride means to them.

Peace . . .

CONTENTS

INTRODUCTION

Sometimes we ride on your horses, sometimes we walk
alone, sometimes the songs that we hear are just songs
of our own.

Robert Hunter

I just got back from another long stint of living in China—
being there takes on many dimensions, much like looking up at the clouds. Depending on where your imagination
leads you, you are at once pondering a dragon and in an
instant, wondering if it will rain. . . . Rain, I hope it doesn't,
for a while at least, because I've got to haul my months'
worth of luggage home on my motorcycle which has been
waiting for me all this time at the Harley-Davidson dealer-
ship. In return for the storage, I had them make a few
"adjustments" to my bike. I've come to accept that's what

you do to Harleys—make them your own, expressions of your attitude about life. There isn't much in our lives that doesn't reflect who we are in one way or another. With a Harley, maybe it's just a little more obvious how we create the world we live in. I added forward controls for more ergonomic cruising and changed the buckhorn factory bars to a wider and lower Roadster style. I put a sissy bar on too since I like to arrive with my passengers where they started and safe. Did I mention new straight pipes and a breather kit for better performance? Okay, so I was away for a long time and seeing as the bike wasn't being ridden, it needed some attention . . . and I needed an incentive to come back to America.

China absorbs me totally. An incredible living dichotomy of a five-thousand-year-old culture facing a massive thrust into a market economy. Their challenge is the challenge we all face—on a macroscopic, societal level as well as a microscopic, personal level. How do we hold on to our traditional roots while responding to change all around us? How do we remain stable and sane while responding to the drive to explore our full potential? How do we keep things balanced and still have some fun doing it? This is "the Ride," with a capital *R*. Discovering who we are in the context of change. The Ride is the metaphor I use in this book for how we move through our life. As the Grateful Dead put it, "What a long strange trip it's been." And it won't stop either; that we all agree on. For me, the Ride is best played out on a motorcycle. It speaks to every aspect of how I see life in that poetic way—the need for balance, confronting your mortality, accelerating, breaking, refueling, tune-ups, repairs, accidents, accepting passengers, and so on. The bike becomes a mirror that reflects the whole of my life.

The Tao (pronounced "dow") is the heart of a Chinese philosophy that talks about living in a natural way. The word *tao* translates as a "path" or a "way," but alludes to an indescribable cosmic order of sorts. Taoism is based on following the rhythms of nature—the rhythms we see in the world around us, and the rhythms we feel inside ourselves.

This philosophy speaks of a way of life based on balance and acceptance. When we look at the Tao of something, we look at its essence, not at its form. It teaches us to perceive a thing's or relationship's natural state and its place in the context of the world around it. Seeing the Tao of anything is seeing its most fundamental aspects. In this way, we break through the intellect, break through the illusions, break through form, break through the commonplace view of something and get down to the truth lying at its very core.

Life has become a drag for a lot of people because society, and the worst parts of technology and human nature, have taken us from our naturalness. A drive for money for money's sake and empty materialism is robbing us of our freedom. We've moved away from the Tao of our life . . . the Tao of the Ride.

It's time to be courageous, and maybe a bit rebellious. It's time to regain our naturalness and freedom. Mostly it's time to start having fun and quit whining. Indulge me on this Ride . . . we journey together.

One

Balance

Don't you cry, dry your eyes . . . on the wind.

Robert Hunter

Every time I sit on my bike and I'm ready to turn the key, I think how wild it is that I'm going for a ride on a vehicle with only two wheels. Sure I understand the physics (as much as our human minds are capable of doing so) of the gyroscopic effect of a fast spinning wheel and the power of centrifugal force. But I still don't take it for granted for some reason; it's too bizarre. I can go back thirty-five years or so when my neighbor Karen, a big, ten-year-old Swedish blonde, "taught" me, a five-year-old, how to ride a bicycle. Her technique (nothing against the Swedes) was to prop me on the big old Huffy with balloon tires while I held the handlebars with all my strength and centered my feet on the pedals. Next, she'd give me a running shove from the top of the driveway of our apartment complex, and I'd be on my way. It all seemed straightforward enough. The faster I'd pedal the smoother the ride. I remember I liked the feeling of the breeze in my face even back then. I felt free—free from the adults, free from all the siblings at home, free like a bird. This sensation lasted all of fifteen seconds before I realized I wasn't free from certain laws of physics, and I smashed squarely into the garage door. Karen hadn't taught me about brakes yet.

Balance goes beyond the ability to not topple over. I see so many people seeking balance who are caught in the duality trap—viewing life as an either/or predicament—falling over or not falling over. I liken it to my initial bike-riding experience. I learned the essence of the Ride lies in balancing the multitude of factors that you face in life. The duality trap—how many times do we see only two alternatives to a situation? Winning or losing, good or bad, black or white.

This is the appeal of superficially understanding Yin and Yang. The Tai Chi symbol, the symbol of the Taoists, ☯, depicts black and white as two opposing forces or aspects or dynamics in any system. One of my favorite and beloved teachers, the ninety-two-year-old Master Duan Zhi Liang of Beijing, hates even looking at this symbol because of what it leads people to think. As a Chinese Qigong healer [*pronounced "chee gung," it's an ancient exercise and healing system—G. G.*] and martial arts expert, Master Duan's true gift is flexibility, both physical and mental, so limits of any kind really set him off. He always speaks of the "perceived" limitation that people construct and how that keeps them from living and enjoying life. Because of this perception that most people hold of limits, they get the wrong idea of life's essence from the Yin Yang symbol. Everything is in a state of flux and chaos, Master Duan would remind me. Gaining balance within this chaos means accepting that nothing is only what it seems. Things are never *just* "black and white." The tendency of human nature though is to simplify and assume comprehension. This is most magnified in the scientific didactic outlook on life. To see two opposing forces at odds with each other is to feed a dualistic paradigm that can dramatically limit your growth and outlook on life.

The *Tao Te Ching*, the twenty-five-hundred-year-old book attributed to China's ancient sage Lao Tsu, is one of the key texts of Taoism. Taoism lies at the core of most Chinese philosophical concepts. It states that from the One comes the great Tai Chi, Yin and Yang, the dark and the light. From this concept sprouts the symbol depicting everything from the Taoist religion and the Korean flag to the surfer subculture. The important aspect to notice on the true depiction of this symbol is the black dot within the white area and the white dot within the black area. I thank my teacher and Taoist friend, Master Wan Su Jian, for introducing me to Master Li at the Shi Fan Yuan temple up in the mountains of Hebei province in China. Master Li's fluency in the edicts, history and principles of Taoism make him a valuable teacher in the area of Yin and Yang. He explains that a seed of dark always exists within the white, and a seed of white always exists within the dark. Viewing life in this way, we can free ourselves from the duality trap—seeing only two sides fighting for superiority—and begin to move toward a much more fluid interpretation of the Universe as we know it. When we recognize the imbedded nature of light within dark, and vice versa, lines of demarcation disappear. More options open in our life. Everything takes on its essential nature of dynamism—as opposed to the static of either/or— and we can feel the infinite nature of existence. To me, *infinite* refers to possibilities. We can't intellectually comprehend infinity, but we can know freedom and that comes with removing the boundaries that define the limits that bind us. Balance lets us see this freedom.

I weave my way down Topanga Canyon, letting the gears of my bike put enough drag on my speed so I can surf down the curves like a bird in flight. I live on top of a mountain in these hills just south of Malibu, and it's one of the great gifts in my life. Easing onto Pacific Coast Highway as the Canyon opens up to the ocean gives me a rush every time . . . the first time I felt it here was over twenty years ago. Mountains and ocean—earth and water—the Chinese consider this balanced relationship good "feng shui," a good interrelationship between existing elements. When elements—seen by the Chinese as dynamic players and not just static objects—are in a harmonious relationship, a good flow of *Qi* is facilitated.

Qi (pronounced "chee") is the word the Chinese use to describe energy in its many manifestations from bioelectric vitality within our bodies to eco-natural movement all around us. Keep this Qi moving, keep it in balance through movement and deep breathing, and health in all its forms is promoted. In the traditional Chinese medical model, pain and disease comes from blocked Qi flow within your body. Get a clog in your gas line and it's no different for your bike. A motorcycle is a good mirror for seeing what goes on inside me. I've always seen life as a mirror in this way: What you see in others and in things around you is a pretty clear reflection of what's going on inside you. Since this is usually a lousy stance to take, most people don't agree with me, but consider a few things . . .

Did you ever wake up in the morning feeling rotten and the first thing you do is slam your toe against the dresser trying to find your lost left sock as you spill coffee on the only clean pair of jeans you have? Then you get on the freeway and nobody is using turn signals that day and you're late for a meeting you don't even want to go to.

Now, what about the morning you wake up exhilarated and in love with everything, you look in the mirror and actually think you look halfway decent, savor your breakfast and find five bucks in your pocket. You get on the road and before you know it, you're at work, someone opens the door for you, everyone gives you a smile, and you cruise through the day like the script was written for you for a change. Hmmm . . . call it chance? I don't think so, though it sure is an easy way out of responsibility. If you don't accept that the world, and what happens around you, reflects your thoughts and your moods, then you don't have to take any responsibility for the world, your actions or your attitude. Isn't that nice?

Responsibility can be looked at as the "ability to respond." My first real teacher of Eastern spirituality, Thane Walker, pounded that into my rebellious eighteen-year-old head when I went to study with him for a couple of years in Hawaii. If life mirrors our inner workings, our hope is to pursue a balance, a conscious resonance between reflections of our outer and inner worlds. As a Ch'an (Zen) Buddhist Master with a respect for the Tao, but who was also trained in Western medicine, Thane taught that this balance is the key to living a full and healthy life. The world is our mirror, our barometer that gives us the reading on our balance, or imbalance as the case may be. If things are lousy, it might be time to stop blaming and begin to take responsibility. It's time to "respond" to the signs around you.

With this viewpoint, balance begins to take on a new framework that expands from the "golden mean" directive of Greco-Roman philosophy. This was a principle that spoke of avoiding excess and living in moderation. The new and metaphysical approach focuses on remaining conscious of how we go "out of balance" as we explore our limits. It's part of being alive to push the envelope, this is how we grow. Sometimes by mistakes and sometimes by sheer willpower. The Tao teaches that it really doesn't matter *how* something happened, just *that* it happened. The trick is to stay awake and aware as much as you can while it's happening. If you get really wasted from partying a little too much, it might be hard to stay awake, but you get the idea. Even pushing your limits in that way doesn't seem too destructive when you know that you're doing it. I only see the danger signs in people when they continually are "out of whack," out of balance and have no clue that they are teetering and preparing to crash.

The way of balance is to stay conscious and responsible for your adventures into the extreme and know what it takes to counterweight the experience. This may be a funny and commonsense way to look at things, but it's wild to see how foreign this is for many people. Seeking balance might mean taking a week or two off from heavy partying. What about taking quiet time to reflect and center yourself when the world just gets to be too much? I watch my friends forget this and wait until they get to that point where they begin to hate the world . . . and maybe themselves in the process. The goal is to balance your view of reality. This view either places your identity within your "ego sphere" or within your "world-you-view sphere."

Another way to see this is to start becoming conscious of the times you perceive yourself as a single person against the world. Then, watch for the times you see yourself as an integral energy working together with everyone and everything around you. By finding the balance between these perceptions, I think we truly start to live. To be free and spiritual at home but bent and tense at work is a painful disintegration. I watch countless people spending half their life being one way and half their life being the other. We can be so context driven, acting one way in front of family and another way with friends, and another way at work. This is what drives us nuts. We intuitively know it's out of balance, but we justify it as the "way it is." I think that's a cop-out. It's just another way we lie to ourselves to avoid facing our fears and frustrations.

There's something about being alone on a bike, cruising down the road in the silence of a loud engine and pounding wind. In these moments, everything can seem perfect. We are elevated from the pressures of life, removed from the responsibilities. No one and nothing can touch us. You begin to wonder why the ride ever has to end, why you have to return to things the way they are. You wonder why the rest of your life can't be like this. Everyone who has something that takes them away from the apparent mundane can relate to this sensation. In those moments of frustration, we feel like there isn't any sense to life; there isn't any balance between the stolen minutes of peace and the chaos of the everyday. In these very moments, I learn most about the balancing act.

Why should your time riding be so coveted? Yeah, I know the obvious, and no one's going to take that private time from me. But why can't I take more of that buzz, more of what happens to my spirit in those moments of reverie and awareness, and infuse it into the rest of my routine? To find this is the essence of balance. It is to know that the ride doesn't stop when you get off the bike.

Balance is about remaining centered. Centered in that place that is our true self. It's about remaining conscious and aware when we are playing roles. In this game of life, roles are crucial to our existence and can be fun when we stay awake while we're in them. When we see we aren't the "roles" but the one assuming them, everything changes. When we maintain balance as we shift back and forth, with both eyes open, we honor our individuality—an important part of the Ride—while being wholly integrated as "role" and "role-player." This is the beginning of the Master's Game, the path of the Sage.

One of my teacher Thane's most influential teachers was G. I. Gurdjieff, the founder of the Fourth Way School and a powerful and unique mystic. He was a seeker who delved into the Eastern philosophies in the early part of this century, way before it became yuppie-fashionable. He taught around Moscow to a devout and secretive following, managing to keep a low profile in the shadow of the czar. Gurdjieff, or Master G as he was known, traveled incognito, dressing in costume and assuming roles. If he were a carpet salesman one day, he'd truly be a carpet salesman, on the street with his wares, in full character. If a student came up to him, he never acknowledged who he was, but simply attempted to make a sale. This was his way of making it known he was in town and, forever the penultimate teacher, to announce there would be a class soon. After the class, held in some sequestered location, the carpet salesman would be seen no more. This is the mastery of roles, to use them for the greatest good, and then to shed them like the empty specters they are.

I hang at the light on the corner of Pacific Coast Highway, every so often a bike goes by, I nod and smile. Everyone knows that ride from Topanga Canyon Boulevard North is made for motorcycles. It's seductive and curvaceous like a woman. Steep cliffs land right on the edge of the road's shoulder on the right and the Pacific falls off to the left. And it's like this more or less to the Canadian border—America's Western perimeter, lure of the romantic spirit and the goal of our ancestors' Manifest Destiny. Well somebody's ancestors'—mine were all living in Italy growing grapes and vegetables up in the mountains.

When my family decided to come to America (they thought it was a decent place, it was discovered by an Italian and named for one, after all), they just reinvented Italy with all their peers. Perception creates reality and they simply created theirs. They kept their language (my grandparents never spoke a word of English even after living in America for years) and their ways intact. They had a fear-based inflexibility, and their survival was based on living as they knew in the old country. I think how that aspect of human nature is still so prevalent today—though maybe a bit less obvious.

Fear-based modalities occur when people fight change and only live within a narrow spectrum of their potential. We find safety in the familiar, we shut out all possibility for change and growth. Clinging to the "me against the world" view, you starve on the few crumbs in your pocket as you sit in the midst of a verdant garden. It takes courage to break out of that pattern. Most of what we've been taught only reinforces the tendency to isolate. This isolation comes from our Western society's skill at developing the ego. The ego, by design, can't see itself as part of the whole because it really doesn't even see the whole. It works on the basis of discrete interactions, making judgments as to where it stands: "Am I more beautiful or less beautiful, more powerful or less powerful, happier or sadder, etc." It sounds a little bit like constant torture to me, but that's what's going on in nearly every interaction when the ego takes the lead instead of your heart. Lead from your heart, as my friend and teacher Joey Bond says.

How do we find and maintain that balance between

retaining our sense of self and living in that joyous place of feeling at one with our world? The first step is to become conscious of how we are off-balance. This might seem easier said than done, but I think not. My sense is that we are all much smarter and more conscious than we let on and that we do a good job at lying to ourselves about it. In the thousands of people I've interviewed and questioned over the years, I'm continually amazed at how acutely aware people are of their imbalance and its roots, yet how unwilling and unable they are to do the work it takes to get balanced. This is a fascinating aspect of the human condition. To be placed in a Universe of infinite potential yet to feel trapped by perceived limitations.

There's an opening in the traffic flowing north up the coast. I let out the clutch, open the throttle, and lift my feet off the ground all in one semiconscious, coordinated movement. That magic balance takes over. In a few seconds, I dance up the gears and my bike and I are smoothly doing sixty. That throaty engine is creating its unique soundscape so many of us find comforting. It's a meditation that may at first glance seem diametrically opposed to my monastic experiences that span more than twenty years. I know in my heart there's no difference between a bike and a temple. I've meditated in some ancient Taoist caves, a day's hike from the nearest town, with some heavy old monks. I can tell you the silence there was more deafening than any Harley. Why do we think "peace and quiet" is necessary for meditation? My friend and teacher, Effie Poy Yew Chow, always emphasized the street noises that permeated her meditation room smack in the middle of downtown San Francisco. To be anywhere in that bustling city was to be immersed in the racket of cabs, trolleys, cablecars and the ubiquitous whistle of the hotel doormen. Dr. Chow said that the noise was a positive feature of that room because it helped us accept things as they were and still find inner peace and focus. I found out later that during her training in Hong Kong, she used to cruise around the city on her own Harley.

This is our world, and our relationship to these stimuli tells a lot about us and our comfort threshold in life. It's not the clamor that annoys us, it's how we relate to it. This applies to everything in life; "noise" can be a metaphor for every annoyance we deal with on a daily basis. One person barely registers the sound of a refrigerator motor whining, while another is driven crazy by it. I watch myself during times when things like refrigerators bug me, and I see the state of mind I'm in. It's usually a time when I need to control my world because I'm feeling a bit out of balance. I observe people who can *only* meditate under precise conditions (silence, a certain crystal, the right incense, etc.) and they fit a personality type that finds security in controlling their world. It extends to everything they do—from work to relationships. Now this isn't to say a favorite meditation environment isn't wonderful; I have mine and I know the power of ritual. I'm talking about situations where we start limiting our ability to be flexible. Our potential as humans is to explore our infinite adaptability. This extends to every facet of our lives. Our minds are fascinatingly amorphous stuff that are truly boundless. Our bodies, with these miraculous hands and their incredible opposing thumbs, can be developed to perform amazing feats from hard labor to finely detailed craft work. Our spirit can comprehend the oneness that is our essence, and it can do it while changing lanes at sixty miles per hour.

I've always believed a motorcycle was a legitimate monastery. I've ridden since I was twelve, and the experience has always been a transcendent one. The isolation brings you face to face with yourself and the danger makes you acutely aware of your mortality. No different than working at a 7-Eleven, just a minor rearrangement of details maybe. The key to balance is to stop seeing differences and start seeing similarities. The *Tao Te Ching* states that when we stop judging the world around us, we begin to see how things, people and ideas are much more the same than they are different. Once we begin this journey, we are flowing with the Tao. The Tao can be translated to "the Way." This Way is what the Taoists see as the guiding principles of the natural Universe. Though Taoists continually remind us that words can't adequately describe the Way, they say if we observe the dance of nature in the world around us, we can begin to understand the Tao. Words can't describe the Way because words trigger our intellect and the intellect is where we operate from a judgment-oriented modality. This is why wordless experiences are necessary to perceive the Tao. Getting on a bike is one of the ways for me.

This is also why music is so important for people, especially instrumental pieces and the advent of "world music." Whatever happened to the great days of rock 'n' roll when every song had a lead guitar part that took you away from the world for a moment . . . and those extended jams in live shows. One of my most intense transcendent experiences was at a Dead show in San Francisco in the mid-1970s. A packed gig in the Haight with people from everywhere. Hells Angels were pushing their bikes down the side aisles so they could be near the stage with their rides. It was lunchtime and the show didn't start for hours, but the place was already full. It was a church and all the pews were removed so it was one big gathering space. That tribal nature of humans took over and we hung out together, travelers from afar sharing common ground. Deep into the set that night, Jerry took off on his guitar during "Eyes of the World" and took us all with him. Jerry Garcia's gift was that he was never performing to *show off*. He was performing to *get off*. His personal experience while playing those jams became a singular event that everyone in the audience partook in. It was a language that needed no translation. That's the power of experience without words.

This phenomenon also occurs when we listen to cultural music, sung in another language that we don't understand. The intellectual brain center that creates words doesn't kick in, and we can savor the experience on an emotional and spiritual level. Silent meditation provides this for so many. I can't emphasize how important this type of exercise is for achieving balance and peace. Countless books echo the same message—as if we need a book to tell us the importance of intentional quiet time. The fact is we do. Life can be so overwhelming we need reminders. Our souls know it instinctively, but that driving ego is usually pretty out of touch with our natural instincts.

Just a little each day. I watch people driving themselves crazy in this modern world. Truly quiet time is so reduced and usually takes the form of driving in traffic or watching TV. Because of our inherent imbalance, these two activities don't fully satisfy our deep need for spiritual rejuvenation, although there is a greater chance that driving in traffic can benefit you over sitting in front of the tube. Traditional sitting meditation like Zen, the sect of Buddhism as it became known in Japan after coming from the original Ch'an Buddhism of China, is not for everyone. Modern living has made it tough to shift gears from the daily grind and settle into a relaxed sitting posture. So many people I know may be able to get over "fidgeting" when trying to sit still, but their minds just won't settle when they aren't focusing on something to do. We've become extremely task oriented in the West. Ultimately, sitting meditation isn't the healthiest activity we can partake in. Crossing our legs in the "lotus position" and keeping our backs erect can block Qi and bloodflow and lead to problems resulting from the ensuing stagnation. The famous Buddhist monk Damo or Bhodi Dharma, who came from India to the Shaolin Temple in Henan Province, China, in 515 A.D., meditated in a cave up in the mountains high above the temple for nine years. He emerged, hiked down to the monks waiting for his wisdom, and told them that sitting in meditation for a long time wasn't that good for them. He devised the early Gong fu (Kung fu) and Qigong (Chi Kung) moving meditations which he derived from various animal forms he observed in nature. Qigong is the ancient Chinese health-care system that utilizes focused breathing to move Qi throughout the body to promote good health and healing. Though the sitting mediation is still the signature of the Ch'an sect (the word Ch'an is derived from the ancient Sanskrit word *dhyana* which means meditation), ultimately the natural movements and breathing exercises strengthened the Shaolin monks into the revered Gong fu fighting force that endeared them to emperors and commoners throughout China.

I think the Shaolin story is an excellent metaphor for the path we all need to follow. Their wisdom comes from the combination of virtuous mental and spiritual pursuits combined with physical agility and flexibility. This discipline of natural balance begs for the integration of mind and body in a conscious way. Westerners are adept at pigeonholing and compartmentalizing life's efforts. Going to the gym or doing regular meditations become discrete events, disconnected from the rest of our day's activities. This is endemic of the schizophrenia that has been pawned off as normal life in the twentieth century. But hey, how can it be considered bad if everyone's doing it?

In my heart, I want to believe that if Damo had a Harley he would have included riding it as one of his "animal forms" of Gong fu. And the Taoists' love of nature would surely endear them to cruising on a Softail. To honor these hopes, it's our challenge to transcend the overt act of driving a motorcycle (or anything we do) and allow it to be what it truly is on a deeper, meta-level. Even from a young age, friends have always said I was too metaphysical. It's my nature to see even the simplest event as an awesome expression of energy flow and consciousness unfolding, so I keep it to myself most of the time. As my old teacher Thane used to warn me, "Don't spook the locals." We lived in Hawaii in the mid-1970s and there weren't a lot of *haoles* (foreigners) around—especially ones exploring the far reaches of human healing potential as we were. "Don't spook the locals" became the term to use anytime you needed to ease someone into understanding or just keep your perspective to yourself.

So many people keep their deeper thoughts and insights about life to themselves, to say nothing of their emotions. Maybe it's because some of the people who do express their viewpoints in these areas are seen as "flakes" or "weak" when it comes to emotional responses or life in general. It sometimes touches an uncomfortable chord in us when someone shares a transcendent perspective if we happen to be in the thick of a predicament. Maybe we're caught up in work, or just overwhelmed by whatever life is presenting us with at the moment. Either way, we don't want to hear about how it all "makes sense" or is an "opportunity for growth." "Kiss this" may be your response of the moment. If it is, I say that's usually the time to go on your bike for a cruise. We only hear the sense of things when we're ready to hear them, so why waste time when you could be riding?

Going for a ride, or whatever your form of quiet time is, certainly shouldn't be escapist. Ultimately, you take all your shit with you wherever you go, and you can't go so far away that you can escape it. Hey, I've tried. Funny how when it seems like you've done everything to change things on the outside—whether it's a new job, new town, new spouse, whatever—if you don't reflect that change on the inside, it's all for naught. The courage it takes to face the real issues and sincerely confront them really sucks sometimes. Whatever the reason for the pain of facing the core of a problem, until we accept it, it's stuck to us like glue. It could be a lot of things we're all familiar with such as the fear of being seen as inadequate, fear of loss, fear of separation, fear of death or the fear of rejection . . . or just holding onto anger. As Pema Chodron, the 1960s flowerchild-turned-Tibetan Buddhist monk, said, "The opposite of acceptance is escape." When I heard that, it rang so true inside me. Whenever we don't accept something or someone, we are being escapist. And in escaping, we are leaving the interaction—the diametric opposite of merging and resolving.

The longer I live, the more I believe that the whole purpose of life on this crazy planet is to learn how to merge, and we do this through loving acceptance. Take it on any level. Maybe for you, what is needed is merging played out through relationships, for another it's merging reflected in serving others. Merging, bringing together disparate parts, may be the journey of self-discovery, figuring out who you are. Acceptance. Learning to take what seems separate—you versus everyone else—or maybe the opposing and conflicting aspects of how you perceive yourself—and merging them through the deepest acceptance of the truth. The truth is that there are no separate things, no separate people. This separation only exists in the delusion of the mundane world we choose to wallow in. In essence, all things are one and we know this intuitively. Oneness comes from that universal energy, the Chinese call it Qi, that permeates all things and, through this penetration, melds everything on an even ground.

Everything is the same in the sense that all things are derived from our perception and, in that way, are reflections of us. Two people look at the same thing yet perceive two vastly different impressions. Sure that thing exists—if it was a piece of wood in the road and you were flying along at seventy miles an hour, your bike would remind you it existed if you consciously didn't avoid it. But the point is that the piece of wood is something different for every rider—and therefore it doesn't exist in and of itself. One rider cruises along, sees it too late because his mind was on his money problems, freaks out at the last second and eats it. The wood was a bad thing. Another rider tools along, cool and present, sees the two-by-four in the road and swerves to avoid it. By changing lanes, she realizes that she moved out of the way of some idiot that she didn't see who, moments later, rearends a pickup truck instead of her bike. The wood was a good thing.

The piece of lumber was real in the sense that it had an effect on the world, but it didn't exist as much as it provoked a response, curiously different, in two different perceivers. The world only exists in relation to who is doing the perceiving. In that way, the world is just a mirror of where we are in that moment. Are we freaking out, or are we cool and present? Looking at it this way, if everything is a mirror of ourselves, then everything is pretty much the same as the next, just a reflection of our state of mind. And if it's all a reflection, then the "world" we see is an extension of who we are. Sounds like merging to me.

We know what those moments are like when we sense this. Everybody has felt that sense at some point in their lives, when it all comes together, even for a brief, but glorious, moment. Everything is aligned, connections are made, you get what you want . . . it's smooth sailing for a change. Merging. It's our natural instinct to move toward this state of awareness on a full-time basis. We are always doing things to merge, to remind ourselves that we're connected to the world around us. We shake hands with people we meet, pat people on the back for doing a good job, make incessant telephone calls, make an issue out of "coincidental" occurrences, etc. When I'm riding my bike and the rush of wind fills my lungs, it's my reminder of merging with nature—bugs and all. So maybe I have a hard time remembering this when a dump truck, on its way to a landfill, is spewing dirt at me and my paintjob. Ultimately, it's another lesson on how I get bent when things don't look "textbook," or at least pleasant. The trick is to accept it for what it is and pass the dude, not to linger in the wake of debris and complain about it.

My bike-riding experiences, like the dump truck encounter, are metaphors that help with all the non-bike-riding experiences. If we agree by now that the world reflects what's going on inside us, then the world we experience on our bike is as legitimate as the world experienced in an office or the world experienced in a 7-Eleven convenience store. The bike is just our choice; everything is our choice. That's definitely a point of disagreement for a lot of people. Most people tell me that it isn't a choice why they're in that job or relationship, it's just a predicament they're trying to get out of or deal with. "It'll be over soon, and I'll get back on with my life," they might say. Saying that things "just happen" pushes you out of the saddle and lessens your responsibility. You end up blaming others and inevitably, challenging experiences keep repeating over and over throughout your life. They repeat like old Morse code signals, continuous sequences of the same message until someone hears it and responds appropriately. It just takes stopping to listen sometimes and choosing to end the madness.

How could it be a choice to be born to an abusive parent or born into poverty or born with a debilitating disease? I'll take a different look at the word "choice" then. We may not consciously choose the details of a situation, but we seem to make choices about how we continue along a path. People in the East talk of karma—the way things from the past bear influence on the present, a massive dynamic of forces that interconnect us with each other and with all our actions. It's not so simple and linear as cause and effect as people may like to think. It's more of a web of connections than a chain of linked events. The crux of it all is that at any given moment, we have the ability to become conscious participants and infuse the situation with enough energy and awareness that we can see the infinite directions that are possible for change. This potential exists in every moment and is always available. Every breath is a chance to change the way things have been going. Every second is an infinite branching point into a possible new future. We just have to have the courage to take initiative. Maybe it's easier said than done, but so what? It's better than seeing the world as hopeless, our lot in life as a curse, and living as a chore. Get over it. When I see myself in that rut, I catch myself and laugh. Didn't used to be that easy though.

In the way that only years of experience can provide, I have come to see the value of keeping a positive attitude. Especially when life turns up the heat, keeping cool, maintaining balance and operating from a centered perspective is crucial to the outcome of a situation. The old Taoists saw the futility in flying off the handle and losing composure. That's the beauty of the great sages and the martial arts masters. It's not so much that they always viewed things positively, it's more that they knew that what and how they were thinking dictated the way things would turn out. Some people like to see life through rose-colored glasses and think you have to stay positive all the time. If my bike breaks down or my finances go down the tubes, it sucks. So what? I'm not going to say it's a positive thing. But now I am more balanced and remember that how I approach the predicament, how I keep my mood in check, makes the difference in the situation. My problem can either be a drag or I can come through it with grace in the fastest way possible.

Another obvious fact that seems to elude us in the heat of the moment is that everything in life returns to its natural state eventually. Balance is a driving force in the Universe. This is the Natural Way of Taoism. Somehow if we can trust this, most of the tension in life fades away. We can stop fighting so much and spend more time facilitating the flow toward balance. It's not that everything eventually ends up in the middle somewhere. It's more like knowing that extremes never last. They always swing back the other way in time.

Thomas Jefferson, one of America's Founding Fathers always inspired me. He was an optimist and believed in the limitlessness of the human potential. At the same time, he wasn't an idiot: When he saw the impossibility of getting anything done with a bunch of Englishmen hanging around the New World, he split for France. There he got inspired by their rebellious Mediterranean spirit and returned to help fight for the independence of his countrymen. He always was dealing with something, whether it was running out of money to build his house (Monticello was a little ambitious) or taking flak for having kids he loved by his well-cared-for slave. Besides all of that and a lot more, he had a focus and a vision and managed to pull it off. My favorite quote of his is, "The harder I work, the luckier I get." This is actually very Taoist when you think about it. He didn't settle for what appeared to be a limitation but worked to change the course of history and regain balance. America was originally based on this premise, to face fear and consciously change things that get out of balance. There will always be courageous people in every country of the world, who rise up and join forces when the balance shifts too far, even when they must look straight into the face of fear.

Two

Fear

When I awoke to Dire Wolf, six-hundred pounds of steel spinning at my window, all I said was "Come on in, don't murder me . . . please don't murder me."

Man's ego (fear) has the propensity to express itself as greed, selfishness and the need to succeed at another's expense. This is the antithesis of conscious living. You can only be truly conscious when you aren't afraid. When you're scared, you create masks to hide behind, maybe the tough guy, maybe the aggressive businessman, maybe the quiet and detached type. You might not associate these three personality types with "fear" but think about it.

Look at fear on a bike. We are confronted by the possibility of serious bodily damage every time we go for a cruise. Now I believe the possibility for danger exists equally in driving a four-wheel vehicle as it does on a bike (see the chapter on karma), but I'll be a bit mundane and simplistic for the moment. Unless you are a jerk, and I've seen a lot out there riding fast motorcycles, you probably respect your machine, appreciate its power and its limits, and cruise down the road within this power/limit grid. Depending on your personality and state of mind, you have your own unique fear threshold. For some people, like me, it falls around fifty miles per hour on wet pavement near the ocean-side S-curves north of Malibu. For others it's 167 miles per hour on the drag strip in Pomona. Still others experience it idling at the traffic light. We all have our fear threshold. If you don't think you do, then I'll guess that yours is with being truthful.

Anyway, appreciating this fear helps us really begin to live. Sometimes I think that people are attracted to motorcycles because of this confrontation with their own mortality; the majority of the population see riding on a fast engine with wheels as a bit risky. I know that when I ride, I face my ability to be "present" in the moment. Maybe it's second nature by now, but I like to feel it for a second, sitting on the bike as it's warming up, feeling how exposed I am, how sensitive the controls are, how close I am to the pavement. It wakes me up and brings me to a place of sheer connection with everything about who I am, my mood, my fragility and my incredible sensory system that even allows me to ride this 650-pound beast. This is the Ride. That split-second sensation that brings you into the present moment, a moment that goes by with a flash . . . yet is eternal. That's what a bike does for me.

The Master's game of Eastern philosophies is all about getting in touch with that "moment." The Taoist sages spoke of connecting with the original ray of energy emanating from the moment of creation. This is a source of pure positivity, as it is only the mind of man that generates negativity. This "ray" is around and within us and is infinitely accessible. Slowing down your mind enough to listen to what's really happening is the key. Appreciating the fear, the elation, the subtlety, the infinite connections, the simplicity, and ultimately, the illusion, is considered the spiritual path in many cultures. The trick is to not judge these sensations, but to simply experience them and listen as you awaken to the truth of your existence. Religious rituals, Shamanic rites and monastic journeys all share this common denominator. Riding a bike can bring us to this awareness. The myriad factors involved in cruising all contribute to this possibility. I know I have a certain "ritual" whenever I get ready to ride. A simple sequence of steps: Slip off the bike cover, swing a leg over the saddle, open the choke, turn the key. You know the routine. This is a sacred ritual, face it. Get into it. Don't rush. It becomes a sensual event that elevates you from the mundane. Connect with it, and you connect with all of who you are.

So you just ride your bike to commute to work and you say it's only transportation . . . or it's just a hobby on weekends . . . or it's just a bike for heaven's sake, get off my case. Well, that's my point. That's how mundane the rest of our lives are as well. If you can't see the awesome beauty of nature, the depth of the Ride when you ride a bike, when the hell are you going to see it? Somehow I'm not convinced that humans can live their lives without sensing the connection with their ultimate nature, with the true essence of who we are. Sure, many people do, but they are the ones who are bitter, or hopeless or numb . . . and ultimately unhappy. Happiness is a real option in this world, not just a fantasy. Sure things suck sometimes, but they are pretty damn good sometimes, too. When we can accept what the Tao teaches us about this, that everything is in a constant state of change and that things can't be judged as good or bad, then we truly begin to live. It's like accepting the fact that you've got to shell out $130 for your five thousand-mile checkup when your bike is running perfectly fine; it's the price you pay to keep things going along smoothly and without a hitch every now and then. It's pretty much common sense, but we still get pissed off when something bad happens. It's not about becoming numb to things that happen, it's seeing them in perspective, as part of that continuum of life, as an expression of the Tao.

You've got to be courageous to look at life this way. To most people, it's either too intense to look at it at all and much easier to avoid any introspection, or it's a waste of time. Since our Western society does nothing to support this kind of thinking, it's no wonder people feel this way. Television is about the best reflection of our society's fear—the advertisements alone point to an inherently inadequate and incomplete people. The only redemption is to acquire the right "product." It's all about fixing the "problem" of our life with some external solution. Sounds like an easy way to avoid facing fears to me. Our life is asking us to accept and appreciate who we are. Appreciate what we have first, before running off to fix something that might not even be broken.

Living in fear takes all the room away, all the room to breathe, all the room to see clearly. I find getting on a bike is one of the great ways to confront my being—the fear and the strength. It helps me see all of who I am. Riding makes room for all of me and all of the world.

If you take the Taoist approach, there is no such thing as a scary or threatening situation. It just is what it is. Every moment is malleable, flexible. This gives us the option to respond in an appropriate way. If we choose to respond with fear, then we just created what it isn't—at least not in relation to the Truth. Even if it is a life-threatening situation, the rules don't change.

Living in Hawaii back in the 1970s put me in some precarious situations. An Italian guy like me with an earring stood out among the locals like a tall palm in a pineapple field. I spent weeks without seeing anyone but locals back then. I was well accepted in our community, but when it was a weekend night and the guys from neighboring towns came around and started drinking, all rules were off. I remember going into this heavy local pool hall to pick up some liquor for a party that we were having. As soon as I walked in, two big Kanakas eyed me up and down and instantly decided to have me for dinner. They were toasted and started sauntering their 350-pound bodies over in my direction, pool cues in hand. I made my purchase and eased out the door toward my car. They were right on top of me, their glassy eyes staring me down, trying to decide what part of my body to break first. I had a whiskey bottle in each hand and thought for a brief moment about smashing them over their heads. I was young, what can I say? But I wasn't scared; I just remember trying to see the situation clearly. When they said they didn't like me and wanted to kill me, I figured it could get ugly. I looked at them, as relaxed as you can be with seven hundred pounds of angry bulk looming over you, and in my heart I forgave them. Then I asked them if they liked playing pool, seeing as they were waving those cue sticks in front of my face. They looked at me quizzically and nodded. I started talking about how my grandfather supported our family during the Great Depression by hustling pool. They looked at each other, then back at me (the only Great Depression they could think of was the one they wanted to make in my skull). I kept talking and said that I'd like to play a couple of games with them, but I had to go. Then I offered them five bucks to continue their game and if I could come back, I would. I'll never forget how they took that bill with their massive paws and just stared at it. That was enough for me to get into the car and scram. Each time I glanced in the rearview mirror as I drove away, I saw the same scene—the two of them standing there, staring at that fiver. My heart was beating pretty fast by then, but it was over. When fear doesn't get thrown in the mix, there is always a clear way through a situation.

Three

Karma

*The wheel is turning and you can't slow down, you can't
let go and you can't hold on. You can't go back and you
can't stand still. If the thunder don't get you then the
lightning will.*

Robert Hunter

The concept of karma has been around for thousands of
years, originating within the Hindu precepts of personal conduct and social interaction in India. Karma is that
wonderful, albeit overused term, that describes cause and
effect, on one level anyway. Rob a bank, go to jail. Simple.
Then there are actions that go without consequence in the
moment, when someone does something bad and gets away
with it. Karma takes this into account too, not to worry.
Some cosmic check-and-balance system is at work that
always delivers the proper blow back to the perpetrator. We
all know about it. For example, some Nazi criminal gets discovered in Colombia fifty years after the fact and has to go
to trial as an old man with twenty grandchildren watching
in horror. Finally, there are the situations where something

horrendous is perpetrated and the villain gets off, scot-free. Fear not, karma has room for this situation too. The afterlife. Where Christianity simply sends you to Hell for the duration, karma prescribes the appropriate return to this life. When you come back, reincarnated, you take on a form commensurate with the kind of life you previously led. In India, the old scriptures talk about this in fine detail. The one I like is that if you steal a pie in this life, you come back as a monkey. You better hope it was a good pie.

So what about biker karma? I see it all the time when I'm riding. I'm cruising along a fine stretch of roadway and some fool in a sedan changes lanes a half-dozen times without using his directionals, basically doing a good job of pissing everyone off. I shake my head and just give him some space so I'm out of his sphere of influence. I just know it's going to come back at him, and low and behold, up near the Ventura County line he's having a roadside picnic with a state trooper. But what about the Cadillac drivers who just refuse to change lanes at all and make you drive around them? I figure they're already paying some karmic debt driving a canary-yellow land yacht, and my mind imagines they had a Harley in a previous life but did something worse than steal a pie. If you need any inspiration to stay on track in this life, that just may do it.

Karma is actually much more complex than this, and though more Buddhist than Taoist (the Taoists prefer to use the term *te* for living with integrity and according to your inner values, or the term *lun hui* which translates to "returning on the circle"), it is a valuable idea to meditate on. All those preceding stories portrayed the linear, cause-and-effect nature of karma. Although that is a part of it, it's not the whole picture. What about how *other* people and things are affected by *your* actions? It's enough to think about what will happen to you based on your previous actions, but how does that energy propagate out and affect people you are in contact with? And since Taoists see energy moving way beyond our conscious sphere of influence, what about the ripples that move from your actions and thoughts into the world, into the Universe at large?

Many stories point to the concept that energy and its effects transcend space and time. Medical biologists are forever curious how various cells in the human body can communicate instantaneously with other cells. These are situations of physiological communication response where it is physically impossible for any signal to be propagated in any known way, be it electrical or chemical.

Dozens of situations in quantum physics (the science that looks at life at a subatomic level) indicate how atoms which are not in contact can undergo simultaneous state changes. Electrons of one atom can exhibit the identical spin changes of another—with no apparent connection between them or the atoms. Calculations show that this information exchange happens at speeds faster than the speed of light, a theoretical impossibility. I like to simply look at a flock of birds and the way they move as one concerted body without obvious visual or audio cues. So many cases show time and space are mere illusions. Look at the phenomenon of distant healing where the patient is hundreds of miles away yet the healer can facilitate almost miraculous cures without ever touching the person. When, at appropriate times, we are able to let go of logic and rational thought, we can open into a more natural place where anything is possible.

The Chinese have a concept called *Jing*. It is a form of energy that contributes to our overall makeup. In some ways, it's like the Western idea of genetics as it carries the energy of our parents and, with it, physical and mental components of who we are. Referred to sometimes as "prenatal Qi," Jing is a tangible thing that connects us to our ancestry and manifests in how we look and act. Linked to karma in this way, we are affected by our Jing and can learn techniques to preserve and improve the quality of this force in our lives. The Taoists have long used the practice of Qigong to do this. They believe the Jing resides in the kidneys and that through various exercises, we can keep these organs healthy. Our kidney system, which includes the prostate gland in men, suffers as we get older and the Jing in our body is depleted. This affects everything from sexual function to hearing. With the proper Qigong practice or related energy exercises, we can stop the tide of this natural deterioration and respond to deficiencies of weak Jing and age-influenced syndromes. This is an example of consciously affecting your karma.

One of my favorite rides is the Redwood Run, a late-spring Harley event in Northern California. This year I started from my home in Mill Valley, just outside of San Francisco, and went to meet a bunch of riders in Novato, twenty minutes north. Not surprising for ten o'clock in the morning, no one was at the bar as planned. I hung around for an hour and still no show. In the meantime, a half-dozen or so beautiful bikes pulled up—obviously a better-planned group. A scarier bunch of hoodlums you'd have a tough time finding. The guys looked like ex-cons, and the women kept a hard edge. My kind of people. I got to talking with the oldest guy in the bunch and he told me he just turned seventy-two and had been riding for forty-seven years. When they said they were ready to split and my pals still hadn't shown, I asked if they would mind if I joined them. A couple of nods and we were off. First stop was to the gas station, as our first leg would take us as far as The Saloon in Wilitz some one hundred miles away. Seeing the look in the eyes of a gas station attendant when a bunch of loud bikes pull up is always worth a laugh. A tortured look of caution and envy for sure. It's even better when they see how cordial everyone is. The old rider even went over and helped some elderly lady in a Dodge Dart fill up her tank. It's fun to confuse people with kindness.

We pulled into The Saloon and found some of the last remaining real estate in the hard-dirt parking lot for our bikes. Well over one hundred bikes and riders swarmed the joint. These runs are like reunions and watching the joy of people grooving on something that they love is inspiring. Loud and inspiring! I talked with various people who shared their woes of blown gaskets and wobbly front forks. Some guy showed up in his girlfriend's car just to hang with his mates. He said he hadn't been able to get his old shovel head running for weeks. A couple more good jobs and he'd be able to buy that carburetor. Another guy slowly got out of the only other four-wheeled vehicle there—a 1957 T-bird. His cane helped his gimp leg support his weight. Lots of people went over to him to see how he was recovering from his latest spill. The old guy in our group hung by his bike as lots of people came over while he held his humble court. It was clear he was respected and liked.

We got back on the road after refueling at the single-pump station next to the bar. This is about as much action as Wilitz gets all year. Riders have an unspoken honor at pumps. Even with long lines of bikers waiting to get their three or four buck's worth of fuel, there's a respect and etiquette that is effortless. At a pump like this, the attendant has to trust you tell him the right amount; you just can't wait to reset the pump for each bike. And riders typically round their payment up to the next dollar amount as a courtesy. This is just the way it's done.

The next leg took us up into the redwoods, an ancient forest of trees over a thousand years old. The two-lane road is carved between these giants so close you can nearly touch them as you cruise by. It takes careful attention as you slalom through the curves. An ambulance came from the opposite direction; we slowed up as it passed. A little later, we saw the debris of a café racer motorcycle being detached from the bark of a redwood.

We were getting close to Richardson Grove, just south of Garberville. The road is a rising grade and rock outcroppings replace the trees for a while. Back and forth we wove. More and more bikes filled the road, everyone giving each other enough room to be safe. I hung back—a vestige of being the oldest brother—as it let me keep an eye on everyone ahead. All of a sudden, my seventy-two-year-old riding partner swerved into the soft shoulder, and his bike was caught in the gravel-filled runoff ditch. Rocks flew in the air, and I put up my forearm to deflect them from my face. He held on—it was amazing he could keep the bike upright. Just then, his right knee slammed into a rock abutment. The bike was repelled back, recoiled, and more shards flew. He was still holding on. The turn in the road tightened and just then he torqued his Dyna Wide Glide back up onto the road, just as the runoff ditch ended in a giant boulder.

I sped up and asked him if he was okay. He nodded, tightening his mouth a bit. For the next twenty minutes, I rode in amazement that this guy survived this. We finally pulled into the campsite, and I asked him again how he was doing. Everyone was surprised because they missed the whole thing since they were up ahead. He said he was fine, but I could see his pain. He limped over to the blankets we just laid down and rested. This is the way of the warrior. He's tough, and this was far from the worst experience he'd been through, he told me. I did a little Qigong healing work on him and the tough group softened and shared a lot of their own stories and interest in healing work. Different members of the group admitted that the knew one system or another, and most of them, women included, were into martial arts. They all agreed that the reason the old guy survived was because he was such a great person. The stories they told of how he helped each of them when they were down were touching. It turns out they all chipped in and rented this bike for him. He really wanted to go on this ride, and his own bike was just stolen.

Karma. Everybody's story is different. Life takes us on a ride that makes us look at who we are.

It's amazing what we carry from our parents in so many unconscious and intangible ways. My love for motorcycles began when I was a youngster, drawing pictures of Harleys and imagining the day when I would get one of my own. I'd talk to my dad about it and he was always a bit neutral, not influencing me one way or the other. When, at twelve, I finally saved up enough paper route money for a little, used dirt bike, I went to my dad to help me get one. At first he was against it, but with my tenacity, he finally gave in. I was jazzed to make this dream come true, and my father got into it as time when on. My younger brother, Jimmy, became the recipient of the bikes I outgrew, and he took to them like a fish to water. He's gone so far as to rebuild antique Indians and is a meticulous bike mechanic and president of his local motorcycle club. One day recently, he showed me an old picture he dug up in my father's drawer. It showed my twenty-one-year-old father sitting on his 1947 Harley. We both had a good laugh about it—something my dad never revealed. Turns out he had several in his day. Maybe an example of how the unseen forces of the past influence us in our present life?

To one extent or another, we've all experienced something that reminds us not to get caught up within the limits of time and space. What about intuition? Haven't you thought of someone you haven't talked to in months, and the next moment the phone rings and it's them? No explanation is available other than something is happening in a way that doesn't fit into the acceptable rules of science. For me, this is a reminder about karma.

If energy can be shown to have effects at great distances—like someone calling on the phone at the same moment you thought of them—then the energy from my actions will do the same thing. How it will affect things, I don't know—and that makes it even more powerful. Your actions, intentions and thoughts move beyond you in ways we aren't sure of. Screw around with this kind of energy, put out bad vibes, and there will eventually be a price to pay. Thinking of things in this way, you don't have to feel controlled or restrained by the rules of government or the police—you must answer to something much more intense.

The good thing about all this is that it works just the same for positive energy. The far-reaching effects of a good deed or a joyful and spontaneous act of kindness are amazing. Watching a completely negative situation turn into a positive one is a trip. It's that bit of magic that we all know. Sometimes I don't think people remember what an intense effect they have on people or things around them. Like flicking a switch, we can change the intention of our heart and mind in a moment, and everything around us will be a transformed. This is known as "guiding the Qi" in esoteric Taoist teachings. It is an expression of karma, the movement of energy (Qi) through our very intention.

The old Sufi mystic, Rumi of Persia, had a wonderful way

of saying this. In one of his magnificent poems, he spoke of hoping that, when walking into a crowded room, good luck would naturally flow to the person who most needed it. Not that he would give it out or even make it happen . . . simply being present in his heart, and joyfully free in spirit, would have a catalyzing effect on the natural flow of energy. Yeah. . . .

Tell me all that you know, I'll show you, snow and rain.

Robert Hunter

The ancient Taoists in China saw nature as the perfect teacher. If life could be lived according to natural laws, then mankind would exist in peace and harmony. Leaders would lead without intruding into the affairs of the nation and people would coexist without fighting. The Taoist belief was that a leader should lead by example, not by force. Taoism came into being at the end of the Spring and Autumn Period of China's history, around 500 B.C., with the writing of the *Tao Te Ching* by the sage Lao-tzu. This was a time when social unrest was high and warlords around the country were beginning to wreak havoc across the land. Taoism continued to grow with the advent of the Warring States Period, which provoked the writings of Chuang Tsu, another great Taoist sage, around 300 B.C. Power struggles were a daily occurrence, and life was unbearable. Cultural growth was at a low, and food supplies were scarce as most resources went into the war effort. China was torn into dozens of separate provinces that basically didn't get along. But it wasn't the people who didn't get along, it was the warlords and the politicians. Some things never change.

The Taoists, inspired by their spiritual guide Lao-tzu, saw that the only solution was to return to a natural way of life. Lao-tzu was the proverbial rebel. If there were Harleys back then, he would have had one for sure—painted black and white, of course. Lao-tzu lived up in the mountains most of the time and stayed away from politics all of the time. He refused offers to take high-paying government posts, laughing at the prospects. As the story goes, he reluctantly agreed to write down his ideas. At the prompting of his followers, at a very old age, he wrote the *Tao Te Ching*, the "book of living by the laws of nature." It is said that he wrote it while sitting on the back of his ox at the gate of the city, preparing to depart on his final journey in this life. It's only five thousand words long but packed with wisdom. Five thousand words that represent the foundation of thought for at least a quarter of the world's population.

Anything that brings us closer to nature and the environment brings us closer to discovering our own inner nature, our own truth. Anything that takes us away from nature weakens our spirit and our body and should be avoided. One of the most powerful concepts in Chinese philosophy comes from Taoism. *Wu wei* loosely translates to *effortless effort*. It is the concept of flowing in accordance with the natural essence of a situation, to merge with a situation rather than come at it with force. To incorporate wu wei when fighting, you use your opponents' force and aggression to overtake them. Rather than meeting force with force, you guide their energy past you and either down to the ground or into an elbow or fist. To apply wu wei at the office, you would take a deep breath before acting and increase your efficiency by sensing what resources are available and guiding energy in the direction of completing your task. Wu wei helps us see that it's not so much that we have a task to complete but a flow of energy to move with. It's shifting our focus so we can get in touch with the process rather than the end result. In this way, we can appreciate the tremendous value in *how* we achieve our goals as much as the goal itself. A seemingly successful achievement can be empty and meaningless if the path taken to get there was shallow and tainted with selfishness or bad intent.

Wu wei is a cool concept to apply to riding. Watch the way different riders take a curve. Some try to overpower the road, banking into the turn with force, holding the handlebars of their bike with all their might. It's not at all graceful, but maybe it appeals to their macho sensibilities, one that supports a tight grip on all things and equates effort with success. Then there are the seasoned riders who float through a turn. They hold on to the handlebars with the slightest grip, even in the hairiest of curves. Their bodies move with the bike like a dancer, the whole process flows like liquid. Wu wei. Don't meet force with force. Resistance only drains us of energy and makes us angry. How many times in the day do we resist instead of using wu wei?

It's obvious that human nature hasn't changed in thousands of years, judging from the ancient Taoist texts.

They are full of reminders to return to a natural state of being, that even in those times was becoming uncommon. In this way of being that moved in concert with the Tao, one faces resistance of any kind as water in a stream meets a rock. It doesn't attempt to push through the rock but instead flows around it. This is the concept that states "soft will overcome hard." That which can flow in a natural way meets resistance in a natural way. Instead of banging your head against a wall, walk around it. When you try so hard to remember something and you have no luck, isn't it funny that when you forget about it, the answer just comes out of nowhere? The Chinese like to talk about bamboo when giving an example of flexibility. When a storm strikes, it is the tall, rigid trees that snap and fall in the high winds. Bamboo is not stiff when it is growing and can thus bend with the wind. Like water flowing around the rock, it moves *with* the force rather than resisting it. It can help us to remember this the next time we face a confrontation. If someone puts up a resistance, try not going head-to-head with them. Sometimes it just takes *not* responding in the expected way to their affront or negativity. Sometimes I just agree and walk away, accepting that that's how they are and not letting it affect me. This is how the water flows around the rock. Ultimately, the water will wear down the rock.

I remember going to Hawaii on my honeymoon. It was over twenty years since I'd been there but I never forgot the October rains. What was a honeymoon without renting a Harley for a few days and cruising the island? But the rains . . . they could ruin those plans. My wife Daisy is fantastic, she enjoys hopping on the back of our bike and hanging with me on any cruise. Her enthusiasm makes me high; isn't that what being in a relationship is all about? We got on our rented Heritage Softail in Honolulu, arranged through the HOG Fly and Ride program, took one look at the dark rain clouds soaking the mountains, and started laughing. What was our choice? Resistance is futile when you're sitting on a brand new bike. The folks at City Harley were so cool and supportive; we hung and talked about life and how there were over ten thousand registered bikes in Hawaii. I had no idea. The biker clubs there are legion. They are family organizations that are generations old. Members are loyal and the bonds are strong. It's the natural way they say; and to them, riding in the rain is good luck. So Daisy and I went off to have some of our own.

Riding in Hawaii is fantastic, and the rain, which could have been a miserable deterrent, turned out to be a great gift. Cruising over the Pali in a light drizzle was almost mystical. This rainforest mountain is magnificent, and the new highway—the most expensive road ever built in the world—takes you right through it. We were immersed in the super-oxygenated atmosphere, bathed in lush greenery like a tropical sauna. Bursting through the tunnel and piercing the mountaintop was a trip, with a view of the other side of the mountain exploding around us. We were drenched, but we were happy. It was one of those times where you realize that even a seemingly lousy situation can be a joy. Winding along the coast of the North Shore where I lived as a teenager, I once again saw the magical waterfalls that

spontaneously appear with the heavy rains. These were
sacred lands to the ancient Hawaiian Alii warriors. In these
mountains, they buried those who lost their lives in battle,
ensuring them an honorable afterlife. Daisy and I circled the
island a bunch of times, moving in and out of downpours
like an amphibian. We'd get drenched as we sliced through
lane-wide puddles and then savored the comfort of that big-
block, V-twin as it warmed us like a gasoline-powered fire-
place. We stopped fighting the weather and just grooved
with nature: on a beautiful bike, like a beast in her domain.

The ancient Taoists used to watch the way animals move
in their natural environments and, from this, they built a
philosophy. Observing the way a hawk circles effortlessly on
the thermal updrafts as it scans for food taught them.
Observing how a turtle conserves its energy and protects
itself taught them. Watching how fish swim with the cur-
rents taught them. To Taoists, living naturally means partici-
pating in the self-governing balance that exists around you.
By moving with these rhythms, our bodies are nourished.
When our bodies are nourished, our minds follow suit.

Building a strong body was foremost to the Taoist.
Enlightenment, on a spiritual level, came naturally by living
a balanced physical life in accordance with the world around
them. Taoist monks, to this day, don't even cut their hair as
they believe this interferes with nature and ultimately weakens them. Through the practice of Qigong's breathing techniques, they strengthen their internal *nei* Qi and external
wei Qi as they return to their natural physical and energetic
state.

With a strong body, you are connected more fully with the Tao, The Way, with Nature. Your mind and spirit naturally follow and become aligned. Through this alignment, you sense the wisdom of the Tao and begin to see how all living things are connected with each other. Through this connection, through this inherent interrelationship, there are no issues about fighting, no issues about need. Sensing and understanding the Tao teaches us that change is the only thing we can really depend on, and in this way, we are prepared, at every moment, to be ready for anything. This sense of constant change leads us to an open and accepting state of mind. An animal doesn't judge situations, it only responds to them according to its need to survive. A Taoist doesn't judge a situation as good or bad because nothing exists in a vacuum by itself. What may seem like a bad incident in this moment may prove to be a fortunate event when you look back on it next week. Same goes for what might appear to be a great situation. Don't get too excited and cocky; what blinds us because of apparent success may turn out to be a big complication later on. The point is, each event, each situation, each relationship, needs to be taken in fully for what it is in the moment. If we can be fully present and nonjudgmental, we can approach a situation with a Taoist clarity and enjoy it for what it is. With wu wei, we respond to it in the most natural way, move with it like taking a curve as if we were a circling hawk.

Each day I learn not to judge events, not to judge people, because the Tao teaches the equality of all things, of all expressions. They are all reflections of the Tao, ever changing. It is only our reaction to these events that makes them what they aren't. They aren't bad even though they may be frustrating or painful. They aren't good just because society agrees with them. They are just expressions of the Tao, of life. How we respond creates them. What actions we take give them life. Anger is easy to see in this way. It's like napalm—it fuels a fire. Add anger to a volatile situation and watch the flames. Add anger to an unstable situation and watch it collapse. Add anger to anger and watch the monster rear its head. Fear is like that, too.

Anger is like a poison that kills naturalness. Animals don't get angry. A lion doesn't get angry before a kill. It's almost the complete opposite. There is such joyous ballet when you watch a predator like a lion make a kill. There is grace and balance, focus and strength. When they overtake their prey, it is almost passionate. The big cats kill so quickly, as if they honor the wildebeest or gazelle and don't want it to suffer, breaking its neck in an instant.

Anger, like fear, blinds us to the true essence of the moment. Anger and fear blind us from seeing what "really" is happening, blind us from what we can learn from the situation. And we only get angry and fearful because we have judged the situation as bad. Judging takes us away from the natural flow.

When we flow with nature, in all its incarnations, we are on a high. Scientists call it the alpha state, that place where the mind is clearly calm and tension is all but nonexistent. This can even be observed and measured on an EEG, a medical device that can detect minute changes in our brainwave pattern and display this value on an oscilloscope in hertz (Hz or pulses per second.) When we are in an alpha state, our EEG shows a signal somewhere between 8 Hz and 14 Hz. According to my engineer friend Richard Lee, author of the book *Bioelectric Vitality*, the Schumann Resonance, the resonant frequency of the atmosphere, at the surface of the Earth is 7.83 Hz. As you move into the Earth's mantle, that layer from twenty-two hundred miles from the core to the surface at thirty-nine hundred miles, the resonant frequency is between 8 Hz and 14 Hz. He points out that, strangely enough, this corresponds to a human's alpha state of calm mental clarity. The conclusion is that when we are calm and centered, we resonate with the Earth. What could be more natural?

Richard's company manufactures a product called a CHI machine that vibrates and emits low-frequency soundwaves in the alpha/earth range. It was developed by a well-known engineer in China named Lu Yan Fang. She researched and tested dozens of energy healers, known as Qigong Masters, to see what they "emitted" when they healed. Qigong is the ancient healing system in traditional Chinese medicine that taps into our inherent energy or Qi field through focused breathing and simple exercises. She found, amongst other things, that they all emitted low-frequency sound waves in the alpha range. She also tested young children, and they naturally emitted the same waves. The device she created with Richard's guidance and vision, now used by over 9,000 doctors in America, has been shown to successfully treat a wide range of chronic pain conditions. There even are cases of people with cancerous tumors that seem to vanish after using this device. It is tremendously effective on conditions ranging from fibromyalgia to sprained ankles.

I'm going somewhere with this, trust me. I'm trained in using this device and even own one, so I think I understand it to a certain extent. Here's the kicker: When you are being treated with it, you feel like you are sitting on a Harley idling at 1000 rpm. No kidding. Granted, it is not as loud or intense, but it has that familiar rumble. Now I'm not about to make any claims about the healing power of a Harley, but it is definitely food for thought that the "natural" vibration of a well-tuned Harley is at once harmonizing with the Earth's mantle and putting its rider into a healing, alpha state. Might explain my attachment after all.

But isn't this just the way life is? We find something that makes us happy, that we groove with, and we are in harmony—with it and within ourselves. It's much more than an intellectual appreciation or, for that matter, simply an emotional attraction. There are resonant connections that we don't yet have devices to measure. This is what nature is all about. Feeling that sense that we are refreshed, rejuvenated, healed. I have dozens of friends who routinely write or tell me about a high they experienced by going to some beautiful spot, or from seeing some awesome display of nature like a double rainbow, or watching the sun set and the moon rise simultaneously, or after seeing a moonbow. It's in our blood, in our souls to be connected with nature in that way: We are all Taoists at heart. Our lifestyles have gotten so out of synch with our inherent nature though that we feel compelled to write about some awesome display of that nature "we see," as if it reminds us of something inside that we feel has slipped away somehow. It's like we are remembering who we really are after a bout with amnesia.

That's what the bike does for me, but I'm not the Buddha. I need reminders all the time to keep me "awake." I try to inspire my friends and students to find what inspires them to remember who they truly are. If it's cruising on your motorcycle, then ride on. If it's pedaling down a bike path in the park, groovy. If you think there is a difference, then I feel sad you can't see the "essence" and you're caught up in the form of the expression [see chapter 6, Illusion]. Nature is enjoyed when we are in harmony with our surroundings. I sometimes think about the noise and pollution a motorcycle contributes to the world. One thing I know, it's a lot less than a car—half the tires and half the gas and oil requirements. Ever see where used tires go? That is an atrocity that drives me nuts. Some forward-thinking entrepreneurs are doing some things about recycling them, but it's evidently a costly process that does more damage than good. The destructive effects of burning fossil fuels is obvious, so when I'm getting fifty-five or sixty miles to the gallon, I feel like I'm doing my part to conserve nature. How many times do you get a holier-than-thou look from some dude in a V8-powered sedan that's getting fifteen miles to the gallon? Okay, enough of that.

The winter weather here continues to be crazy. Seventy-five degrees and sunny by day, then, when the sun sets and it starts to get cold, the beach areas fill with thick, wet fog.

Then the fog rolls up the canyon and fills it like milk being poured into a bowl. The canyon fills up and the house where I live gets engulfed . . . what a trip. . . . And tonight, after helping friends move—loading a big van and then unloading it across town over the course of the day—and my artist friend Tim has seven thousand old vinyl record albums!—after that, I had to ride the bike home in the pea-soup atmosphere. Intense, with zero visibility, it was like I was shining the headlights into a mirror three feet away. The road was slick, like snakeskin. At the last leg up to my house, way on top of the ridge, where the road is almost vertical, unlit and unpaved, I just said into the darkness, "God, please help me tonight" and it was awesome. I blasted right through the fog layer, going up so steeply and so quickly. I got to the top, to my house, and looking around, it was like the bike and I were floating just atop a sea of dense white fog that extended in every direction. The only other thing I could see was the mountain range a couple miles across the canyon, peaks emerging like icebergs, penetrating toward a sky slowly filling with stars . . . heaven's grace for another trippy ride.

When the wind is in my face, piercing every cell in my body and my senses are so acute I can smell every flower, every pine needle, take in every detail going by me like in a dream . . . when I can feel the pavement texture through the spinning tires and know what a panther must feel as she blazes through the jungle, that's when I remember. Riding does that for me. It's a trigger . . . a kick in the proverbial ass to wake up, wake up from a sleep that is taking humans away from their humanity, from their connection with the world around them. I wish for everyone to find that thing that enlivens their senses, that wakes them up . . . to remember . . . to know their place in nature.

Since it costs a lot to win and even more to lose, you and me bound to spend some time, wondrin' what to choose.

Robert Hunter

When you ride a 650-pound machine that can easily go one hundred miles an hour, I pray you have well-tuned senses. Not just the five we're used to—seeing, smelling, touching, hearing and tasting—but also that extra-sense that keeps you from the real trouble.

Training with the monks at the Shaolin Temple in the Song Mountains, and with my ninety-two-year-old Wuji wushu teacher Master Duan in Beijing, I learned a lot about the senses. In China, the ancient Masters didn't separate the senses from the mind or spirit; they didn't separate fighting from healing. The same energy, Qi, used to defend yourself and subdue your opponent can be used to heal someone with an illness. The physical body reflects the spirit and the spirit reflects the body. Everything in life is an expression of the Tao, of the law of Nature, the continuum of energy that began at the moment of creation. That energy can be tapped into as if rays extending from that moment of singularity.

When matter and energy were one and inseparable, it was called *Wuji*. Wuji translates to something like *infinity* or *the limit of non-beingness*. Master Duan looks at it like that moment right at the edge of creation, that first breath God breathed into the world as we know it. From this oneness of things came duality, the Yin and Yang of the Great Tai Chi, darkness and light, hard and soft, all opposing and complementary forces. From these forces emerged the *Bagua*, the image of *eight directions*, the physical and mental world as we know it. For this, we need our senses. As humans, we spring from the union of heaven and earth, from the Yang forces of heaven and the Yin forces of earth. We are the product of this melding of energies. When we honor this union, we can flow with the Tao, with all of nature, the nature in all things. Our senses are all we have to respond to this ebb and flow of life. Our five base senses connect us to the physical world; our intuitive sense connects us to the Universe. They've got to work in harmony for us to be whole. Weighted too heavily on the physical and we become mundane, materialistic and competitive; weighted too much on the ethereal and we can become disconnected, despondent and ineffective. To find that balance in who we are is the gift of this life. Within this balance lies the Tao.

Imagine if we can elevate our five physical senses so they penetrate the intuitive, spiritual world. Imagine if we can elevate our intuitive senses so that they can work together with our physical senses. This is one of the keys to truly flowing with the Tao: We eliminate the lines of demarcation; we erase the barriers to how we define ourselves. It is at the core of the mind/body argument, a debate that started even before the Greek scholars like Aristotle and Socrates waxed on these issues. Growing evidence suggests that the West and the East mixed during this time. From Hebrew herbal remedies that called for plants that only grew in Asia, to Chinese olive oil remedies they must have adopted from Mediterranean sources, we continually see new evidence showing that ancient peoples intermingled. Socrates referred to a great red Phoenix, clearly a Chinese symbol. This all simply means that world peoples have had enough cross-pollination to show that it is a fundamental human trait to question the essence of who we are. Mind or body; senses or spirit.

Ultimately we can't live without either, so we must be both. The question then becomes, can either operate successfully separated from the other? This is what makes people crazy—to experience the physical senses without being sensitive to our intuitive, spiritual nature, or to experience our higher self without grounding it in the physical. Sex seems to be that place that can accelerate our awareness to a point where we can melt the differences between physical and metaphysical. We are vulnerable enough to be receptive, the ecstatic experience at once enlivens our body and takes us out of its clutches. Ancient Taoist texts place heavy emphasis on using the sexual experience to build our Qi and heal. Conscious lovemaking can lead to "dual cultivation" where each partner participates in balancing the Yin and Yang forces of his or her lover. Intercourse becomes a powerful meditative event that transcends simple physical pleasure and brings both partners to a deeper connection with each other in the Tao. The physical senses and intuitive senses merge. There is an alignment within each of you and a harmonic is created that aligns you both. Though this takes practice through various exercises such as shared breathing and ejaculatory control, the results are well worth it as they strengthen and heal both of you, and at once, the relationship.

The trick to understanding the relationship between physical and intuitive senses is to learn to get more in touch with that perception of experiencing both worlds at once. The shamanic religions walked this line. They used techniques like chanting, dancing and psychotropic plants to break down the hold we have on reality—a reality that needs an ego to clearly define the physical and nonphysical worlds. The Buddhists used secluded meditation and mantras, repetitive prayers, to break their ego hold. The Christian religions placed the focus on God to take humans from their focus on their own egos. The Taoists saw all life, everything, as an expression of the Tao and through this homogenization, left no room for an isolated self.

What do we rely on in this modern world to create the ecstatic experience to take us to this place?

My theory is that everything we do can be this catalyst. It simply takes shifting our perspective and attitude to get there. We've become so numb to the melding of the physical and nonphysical that material and spiritual are socially accepted as separate entities. You go to work, and you go to church. Two separate and disconnected events from opposite ends of the Universe. This basic assumption just mirrors the questioning that goes on inside us—that the physical and spiritual are mutually exclusive, that they can't easily coexist. Imagine, though, that we can do something as mundane as riding a motorcycle and thus perceive it in context of an ecstatic experience. Of course I am being facetious about the "mundane" part—just trying to prove a point.

I think bikers are hooked on riding when, in a moment, the experience links them to the "ecstatic" and transcendent aspect of the ride. You might not get every biker to articulate it that way, but the essence is there. Talk to anybody deeply hooked on something they love and sooner or later, you'll hear them talking about how their senses are awakened and it's like a "religious" experience. I've heard this in the context of golf, tennis, jogging, swimming, mountain climbing, surfing, knitting, painting, calligraphy, dancing—you get the idea.

For me, it's getting on the Harley and taking off up some canyon or onto the freeway headed anywhere. That's why this book is what it is. But it's just a metaphor, a trigger to inspire you to find your muse, find what brings you to that transcendent place where your senses move beyond their physical prisons and wake you into your true self.

I get on my bike and I am fully in my body, the noise and the vibration won't let me forget. My senses become superbly acute as I assess the world I am about to ride into.

I am so fully physical, so fully emotional, that I am beyond their grasp. I am out of my cage; my perception is heightened from the survival needs of not only the physical body but of the spirit. For your spirit, your soul, to survive, it must be nourished. And the nutrient that it needs is freedom—freedom from the illusory grasp that the body has on our self-perception. When we loosen this grasp that takes us out of a physical-dominant self-view and move into a more balanced body/soul perception, our soul flies and is free. You know the times this happens for you. My hope is to simply make these moments more common, and to make them attainable at will.

Find your groove. Find what turns you on. I write about the Ride in relationship to a Harley. That's just as legit as someone describing the Ride in the context of windsurfing or playing music or painting or cooking. It's the process; the details are immaterial. Get caught up in the details and you see why people fight so much, judge so much. Let go of the details, look beyond the illusion of the senses, and you are on the path to freedom.

Illusion

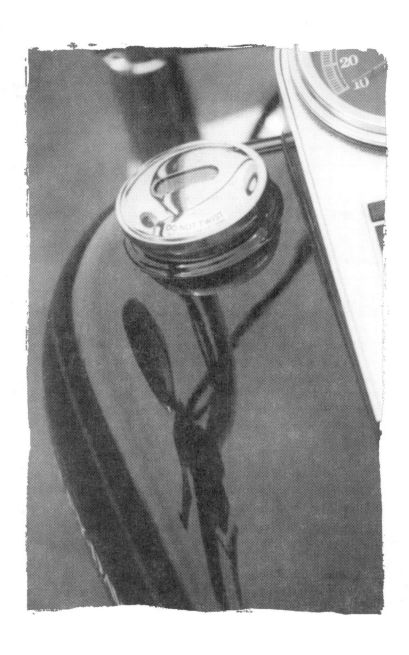

I know you rider, gonna miss me when I'm gone, gonna miss your baby from rolling in your arms.

traditional American song lyric

An old Zen story tells of a great master who dies suddenly. His closest disciple, also a greatly honored master, sits next to the body for two days and cries and cries. This really frustrates the monks of the temple as one of the edicts of Zen Buddhism is to practice detachment and to understand the illusory nature of all things. Finally, when the monks could take no more of this crying from their great master, they sent the eldest to confront the situation. The elder monk asked the master how could he cry so if death was just an illusion. The master looked up with his bloodshot, teary eyes and said, "This is the saddest illusion I have ever experienced."

A true master doesn't get stuck on the rules . . . or on the illusion itself. True mastery comes from being completely who you are in the moment and to understand the nature of illusion. If you are sad at the "illusion" of death, how dishonorable is it to not weep? It's like talking about the illusory nature of life, while at the same time, making sure not to stand in oncoming traffic. Life is illusion to the extent that it is created by our reactions to it. It's all an illusion in the sense that there is not *one* reality, but an infinite, dynamic reality that moves with our perception, that changes with the perceptions of others. How we *respond* creates reality.

You get on your bike. You start the engine. It purrs like a beast. Sure, on one level you are just riding a motorcycle. Is that the whole story? It can be, I imagine, but that's the limiting view that makes life mundane and miserable. Do you have the courage to see what else is going on? How the event is reflecting so much more in the process? For me, it shows me how balanced (or unbalanced) I am, what state of mind I'm in. The bike is the mirror—it presents me to myself. It presents the rider to the Ride. I see how in sync I am with my emotions. In that moment I feel how strong I am, how healthy I am. And like a good mirror, it almost magnifies in its clarity. I am taken out of just being a body on a machine and put into an event, into the process of the Ride itself. I'm not a guy on his way to teach a class; in that moment, I'm an infinitely conscious creature expressing itself, unfolding and expanding as it remembers its connection to everything . . . and nothing. I am potential energy, a probability wave that can be guided and directed with my conscious intent . . . limitless.

The ride is a rush. You are so completely consumed that you are free from the trappings of life. No financial pressures, no relationship hassles, no responsibilities. You grab hold of both handgrips and at once let go of everything you left behind. The noise is louder on your bike, yet it is a relaxing silence. The wind growls and shrieks, but it is still. The roadway pounds and the hours strain at your flesh though you are comforted. What more can show us the illusion that we've bought into in this life? What can be irritating noise in one context is heavenly music in another. When our mind is engaged in what we love, we transcend the illusion of things. How can we take this into our world when we turn off the engine? We must understand that the ride never stops. Imagine what it would be like to feel that connection to nature we get when we're cruising . . . while sitting in the office? This is to live in harmony with the Tao. It is to transcend the illusion of the ego.

The ego, our image of isolated individuality, creates fear from its sense of being a separate entity, apart from everything else. To have the courage to break from this spell society has cast on us, to express our true freedom, is the hope of everyone. Ultimately it requires breaking down the illusions we hold of ourselves. My buddy, Michael, and I were in a ritzy neighborhood today and we got so pissed after being there awhile because of how the people acted. There is that sense of "me against the world" when you see these people act. The way they primp separates them from the world. The way they push themselves around without regard for others separates them from the world. The way they get out of their fancy cars leaving their door wide open to passing traffic as they double-park and block passage separates them from the world. They seem to separate themselves from the world so they can confront it, and they confront it in order to succeed. This is a common behavior in competitive personalities. We didn't loathe them for their money, just for their disrespectful attitude. And then we didn't actually feel anger as much as sadness.

The illusion they hold of the world as an adversarial jungle, made up of other disconnected individuals all trying to succeed at their expense, is what perpetuates the disease. Buy into an illusion, and you've got your reality. It will be as real as your hold is on your illusion.

Somebody all decked out in jewels while she is doing her grocery shopping pushes her cart up to me in an aggressive manner, not even looking up. When she finally does, she sees some unshaven guy, dressed all in black, dark shades with a helmet under my arms. That look of disgust comes over her face as she sizes up her adversary. I slowly pull off the sunglasses, look at her and smile. It disarms her. She gets embarrassed and begins to apologize profusely about almost decking me with her cart. Deep down she knows she was just imprisoned by some illusion moments before, and it wasn't who she really was. I nod and she passes. So what if she goes back to her previous behavior? In that moment, something was released, some part of her armor was disassembled. This is how we confront and change illusion—using something as simple as a confidant and sincere smile that talks to a person's soul and not his or her image.

The ego survives under the illusory masks that we wear each day, and we may have many. Each mask, like the layers of an onion, separates us from our true identity. Somehow we feel that revealing our true identity makes us vulnerable and unprotected. In some ways, it's true. So what? What becomes vulnerable and unprotected is in point of fact the ego and not our true nature. How can that essential self ever be touched or hurt? It can't, but the ego can be. Since so much of the ego's game gets played unconsciously, we are rarely in sync with it, and it therefore seems intangible. We just hold on to what identity we think is real, and fight to maintain it. We then identify with some image, some specter of who we think we are. It may be our professional role ("Hi, I'm a designer") or our protective role ("Don't worry, I'm always this quiet"). These are the masks we wear to help us cope with the fact that we think we can't fully be ourselves. The Master's Game is to become conscious of our masks. Learn to get in "sync" with how and when we use these masks. Yes, they are protective and sometimes necessary. When we can pull their use into a conscious place, we become free of their hold. But, like Amelia Earhart said, "Courage is the price life extracts for freedom." It takes courage to be free enough from the hold the mask has on you. Once you are free, though, you can begin to have fun with those masks.

I teach Qigong a couple of times each week. Whether it's in Santa Monica or Malibu, the ride out the canyon and along the coast is incredible. At first, the image that the new students build of their teacher who rides up on a loud Harley is completely prejudiced by their preconceptions of what a "biker" is all about. A few students, after having the courage to return to class several times, come up to me and tell me how different I really am compared to the guy they thought I was when they first met me. Some even go as far as to say that I've changed a lot over the weeks. The illusions that we carry in our minds about the world around us are fascinating. They are uniquely our own, molded by the myriad inputs and authorities we take in during our lives. So does that mean everyone lives in his or her own private illusory world, coming together on some common ground that we all have agreed upon is reality? Sure. Shamanic and religious systems are predicated on this assumption. So are advertising campaigns. Scary, huh? The goal of understanding illusion is freedom. It's the payoff for coming to terms with the malleable and amorphous nature of life. If we can accept the fact that all we experience is an illusion—an illusion to the extent that we build it based on a set of arbitrary rules that we have allowed to be real—then we are approaching that moment when we can truly begin to live. At that moment (and there may be many throughout your life), when you accept the fact that there is no fixed reality, no hard and fast set of rules that need to be followed, no limits or borders, you are making the choice to be free.

Seven

There is a road, no simple highway, between the dawn and the dark of night, and if you go no one may follow, that path is for your steps alone.

Robert Hunter

J anis Joplin sang her song of freedom some thirty years ago to a searching generation. Maybe she sang it from a more bluesy place, a more rebellious place, than a Taoist perspective may relay, but Lao-tzu probably would nod in agreement. When you have let go of everything that you cling to for safety, you are free. When you lose your balance that only comes from a tenuous hold on unstable handles, you are free. When you shed the images of who you think you are, you are free. When you shed the restraints that come from what other people expect of you, you are free.

Isn't that one reason why people like to ride motorcycles? No restraints, no safety net, nothing to hold you back? An image of singularity, independence and total connection with the Universe . . . freedom. It's not the only path to this experience, it's just one that works for me and the others that groove with it. The question is, what's *your motorcycle*? What promotes your freedom? What's your Ride?

These metaphors of life all paint the same picture. They all converge on freedom. If you aren't free then you are constantly trying to escape. I see it all the time in people. It's the "thank God it's Friday" routine, the mass exodus on holidays, the constant need to "get out" of something or from someone. The Tibetan Buddhists counter the opposites *acceptance* with *escape*; from this, we can equate freedom with acceptance. To be free, you must be able to accept things and people for what and who they are. It doesn't mean you have to like them or even agree with them. It just means you don't change who you are because of them. It means you don't create adversarial relationships with things or people just because you can't accept them. Freedom comes with detachment. Not identifying with something or someone who upsets you means that you know they can't ultimately affect you, that who you are is completely free. Okay, so what if someone gets in your face or hurts someone you care about? A Taoist would simply do the most efficient thing to balance the situation. I'm not telling you how you do it, just do it and move on with living.

That's the point of freedom. Don't cling to negativity; it's just a sign that you can't accept something. Let it go. Let it be free and you'll be free. It may mean breaking ties with someone whom you imagined should be with you. It may mean getting rid of your dream house. It may mean giving everything away and moving to another country.

Each of these things I've had to experience to learn the

lessons I needed in this life. Each time I was released from a self-imposed entrapment. Each time it took courage to let go and in so doing, I discovered the truth of who I was. I was guided by my heart and not by what I felt was right by society's logic and standards. For the past two years I've been living in China, having left everything secure behind to follow a dream. With no preparation or plan, I went only with the trust that this was the "right" thing to do. I *knew* I'd meet my destiny, probably in the form of some teachers who'd guide me on my path of healing and the martial arts. It must have been the right thing for my soul because the Universe came through in ways I could never have imagined. Sometimes it takes these extremes to end non-productive patterns in our lives. Sometimes it may mean just getting on your bike and going for a long ride. . . .

Cruising for hours through the flatlands defined by endless mountain ranges that stand watch like ancient sentinels, they kiss the heavens as their peaks turn white with snow, I'm tethered to that high, breathing in this air as I fly over the earth at ground level. Los Angeles moves farther away, taking its foul air with it, leaving me colder, but invigorated. The Harley seems to ride even smoother somehow as the desert moves closer and closer, that powerful expanse brings with it the unique sense of freedom that only twenty-five-mile visibility can elicit. It reminds me of Tibet, standing out in the tundra and being lent the gift of vision, a clarity unmatched, for at thirty-five hundred meters above sea level, the air is truly invisible and with it, distance disintegrates. It is the most tangible sensation that time and space are folly, illusion. Freedom from this imprisonment, even for a moment, is a treasure that can be carried back with you to temper daily life. You are transformed and can then share it with friends.

Then, cruising through the desert, another illusion breaks—the California/Arizona border. It's like going through an invisible veil, where bikers pull over and pull off their helmets. State laws, like all laws of man, are arbitrary impositions. I think of this twisted game as I secure my half-shell to my sissy bar and tie on a bandana. Freedom. Feeling the wind whip around your head unobstructed, shedding the weight of all that plastic, eliminating that wind resistance that wrenches your neck, yeah. Lots of riders choose to wear helmets all the time, and that's cool, but bless Arizona for giving riders the choice.

The desert is far from desolate. Saguaro cacti show their imposing presence in your peripheral vision. At seventy-five miles an hour, the desert blur is unique in and of itself. Wildflowers jump out from the sand. This winter has been wet and the earth shows its gratitude. On a bike you are engulfed, immersed in this opera, a participant, dancing with the world around you. Your rearview mirrors become animated postcards teasing you with their beauty. I pull into the modern oasis, better known as Loves Truckstop. Their twenty pumps are refueling everything from dirtbikes to massive RVs. Anybody out here this far in the Mojave is an explorer of sorts. Getting away from something old, heading toward something new. Three bucks fills me up and I slide my bike into a space flanked by dozens of others, mostly full dressers this far from civilization. Two couples in their late-fifties sit near their black Electraglides enjoying their lunch. I squat near them and we share the beauty of the day, laugh at the absurdity of any other way to live, and wish each other a safe ride. It's this kind of brotherhood, spanning generations and cultures that is so infectious, so cherished amongst bikers.

Cruising isn't for everyone—but then, neither is freedom. For a million reasons, many people don't choose freedom—or don't think it's even an option. You know where you are on this issue; no one has to tell you. They can't anyway; the path to freedom is a personal one. Freedom takes choices, decisions, sometimes difficult at that. Freedom isn't about what you do, it's how you do it. I know mothers with four kids who are more free than a single guy with a new Fatboy. Don't get caught up in image and form, thinking that some "thing" or lifestyle will bring you freedom. That can be a lonely and fruitless journey. Freedom exists within this very moment. It's only a decision away. When you make that choice, everything changes, the very matrix of the fabric of your existence is rearranged. When it does, you can never go back. True freedom affords a perspective upon which everything else is compared. Once you've tasted it, nothing else can exist without being viewed in relation to it. Eat a piece of melt-in-your-mouth Italian chocolate then try to tell me how much you still like Hershey's.

That's what long cruises are like for me. Everything I do when I return is transformed by that experience. I honor the most mundane activities; in fact, they are no longer mundane at all. Blazing down the freeway at seventy-five miles an hour, the slightest use of your brakes, the way you change lanes, all must be done with a consciousness, an honoring of preserving your life and others' on the road.

Back home, I take a new care in my actions and gain a new appreciation for the subtleties of life. Things become precious. Your freedom in turn frees everything and everyone in your life. They are no longer what they appear, they seem to have changed somewhat, and can truly be something beyond those limitations. They are free to be, to express, their infinite and essential nature. Your freedom is contagious.

The Taoists agree on one truth: Change is the only thing you can depend on. It is the core of all life. The constant movement of every bit of particulate matter that the quantum physicists speak of is very Taoist. Scientists constantly discover that nothing is what it appears to be, that even the most solid-looking matter is made up of mostly empty space and what tangible stuff that is there is moving in such a way that it can't fully be quantified. The Taoists accepted this twenty-five hundred years ago. Accepting change is true freedom. Allowing change is the sign of a sage.

Real freedom is threatening. Real freedom is a tough thing for people to accept. It challenges the very fear that is at the core of our fragile human nature. There are so many countries that don't allow their citizens to be free, while in others, freedom on this level is taken for granted. But what about the freedom you personally experience, that you allow yourself to express?

The ego survives on constraints, on rules, on definitions, on borders. The ego (our "essential fear"—try using this term instead of the word "ego" in any sentence, it works the same) depends on a clear-cut, unchanging reality to allow it to flourish. The ego is predicated upon what external things (cars, houses, relationships, etc.) exist to define it, to feed it, to nourish it, to allow it to grow. When the ego becomes bigger than our ability to discern it from our true nature, then we are no longer free. You can't survive without the ego, at least not in the world as it is today. Maybe in a protected monastery the ego can appear to be extinguished, but not in the world I see. So if it is in fact essential, at least work to keep it manageable. In so doing, you'll be free.

Every day I look at what I think is indispensable in my life, what I feel I couldn't live without. When I admit what it is, and sometimes it's not easy, I try to ask myself why it's so. It's a great exercise to see what you're holding on to. Granted, some things are practical issues, but I consider them anyway, the ego is an insidious creation and very tricky at that. Sometimes I give things away that I thought were essential, and it's freeing. Especially if I became particularly attached them. Everybody knows how good it feels to let go of anchors that tie you down. Even if you don't carry through with giving something away, sometimes just coming to terms with why you cling to it achieves the same goal.

It's not the form that an action takes, it's the intention that drives it. The Tao will show us when we are acting in a natural way. It "feels" right. We inherently know when we're being "fake" because a voice in us tells us. We may not choose to listen to it, and when we don't, we feel lousy. This is an example of living in an unnatural way. When we are caught up in "form," we are reminded of how trapped we are. These "empty actions" keep us in jobs or relationships that are not right for us; we stay because we feel we are supposed to. It drives people to buy fancy bikes because they're a status symbol. These are heartless actions that keep us in a prison of illusion and lies. Freedom from form keeps you from being tied to any set of illusions, even altruistic ones.

I just sold my bike. I've had it for a while and was getting attached. Some guy really liked it, so I gave it to him for a song. He was elated and I faced, once again, my attachments and theories on formlessness. The nomad in me has awakened, and I'll leave this town I love and feel so safe and peaceful in . . . and move to a cold northern city in bitter winter. This seems to be my life lesson, to let go, to forge ahead into uncharted territory, away from things when they get too easy and safe. I move into that place that frees my soul, that wrenches faith from its deep cavernous hideaway, to remind me that there's another bike waiting to be bought. It's another acknowledgement that change is constant, that the infinite nature of the Universe expresses itself with brutal clarity and unbelievable variety. I stand once again on the precipice and feel the warm and icy gust of freedom in my bones. . . .

When we can live freely, we inspire those around us. Freedom is contagious; remember Eastern Europe in 1989? Problem is, fear and the ego are just as contagious—that's one of the dichotomies and quirks of human nature. Be free, promote freedom, inspire freedom. The ancient Taoists in China savored their freedom. They refused comfortable government jobs and remained in austere mountain enclaves to protect their freedom. They constantly bucked the regimented social system to protect their freedom, their freedom to discover and pursue the truth of who they were, the truth of their lives and that of their family, and the good of the community as a whole.

Though the Ride is ultimately an individual experience, it can't be done alone. This is the paradox of life on this planet. We only discover the truth of who we are through others. It always takes others to help us uncover our potential. The brotherhood that exists among riders is legend. How such a solitary event as riding a motorcycle can foster community spirit, deep ties and friendships is astounding. I constantly see how bike riders find their personal freedom through being responsible to the club or group they belong to. This appeals to our most basic tribal instincts. I just heard about how an enormous group of Turkish bikers on the island of Cyprus just stormed the Greek border in a life-threatening attempt to make a political statement. They acted from their sense of duty and faced a hostile army aiming machine guns at them. Everywhere I travel, I discover that bikers have assembled and created associations to further their interests, whether it's to go on group rides, become politically active or just honor the brand-name bikes that they have become attached to. The Harley-Davidson Owners Group (HOG) alone has over four hundred thousand members worldwide, made up of local chapters everywhere you can imagine. These groups raise millions of dollars for benevolent charities around the world with their "runs," or group rides, that members make donations to. The causes range from giving toys to orphans at Christmas to raising money for cancer research. Not bad for a bunch of leather-clad hoodlums that you'd rather not meet down a dark alley. So much for image. But as the Tao teaches, nothing is as it appears.

The ancient Taoist sage Lao-tzu is always shown riding an ox . . . but I'm sure that if he had the choice, he'd be on a Softail.

Eight

Thoughts from the Road

Wake up to find out that you are the eyes of the world.

Robert Hunter

The following pages are really where this book begins. I asked a bunch of riders from around the world to share what *their* personal motorcycling experience was; what the Ride means to them. The actual question I posed to each person was: *What is it about riding your motorcycle that feeds your soul, and how does it help you cope with the rest of your life?*

What I love about people is that we are so different in detail but so similar in essence. Each response reflects exactly *who* the writer is . . . not so much in the words they used but in how they approached the question. This is the magic of being human. We each interpret the world in our own unique way. What we give back is just what and who we are. From Dr. Martin Jack Rosenblum's poem he most graciously created for this book recalling a time gone by, to Amy Holland's experience from the very week she wrote her response, our perspective on the world is ours alone. Time and space are irrelevant. Even the words we use are only vessels upon which we carry our intention. What we get from reading personal experiences like these is more of a "feeling" than actual facts. It's the stuff between the lines that touches us, that triggers us. The "way" people express themselves is what talks to our intuition, what tells us who they are. I never listen to only "what" a person is saying, but more to what I'm feeling beyond the words. Words rarely convey the truth we are hoping to share.

The philosopher Wittgenstein once said, "We are bewitched by our words." He also said, "We live in a word-built world." The conclusion you might draw is that it's all pretty hopeless. I'd rather put it all in context of the Tao. There is a balance that we can attain which will allow us to be in this world of words without being limited by them. The key to this balance is living from your heart.

I hope you enjoy the following heartfelt words as I have. Listening to the passion and joy that rides between and within the words on the pages that follow takes you on a personal journey, yours through the experience of another. This is the key to inspiration. Each rider has helped me create this book, to bring a dream to reality and to allow a percentage of the proceeds from its sale to be donated to a variety of charitable causes. My belief is that we are here in this life to inspire each other, to strengthen each other and to remind each other that we are all on this Ride together.

Peace.

MARTIN JACK ROSENBLUM, Ph.D.

Age: Fifty-two

Occupation: Historian, Harley-Davidson Motor Company

Home: Shorewood, Wisconsin

Years Riding: "I got rides as a mascot of sorts for a bikerider club in the mid-fifties and began riding myself in the late-fifties."

Degrees: B.S. in English and History, M.A. in Literature, Ph.D. in American Literature, History and Culture

Secret Lingo

It was bikeriders then
Not bikers (which came later)
And the ride was not with much
Chrome (mostly blacked-out and bobbed)
But it was all the same
You would do the job all week or sit in classes
And by Thursday the bike would be
Prepared with
The kind of care
Deserving of a fine
Guitar before a gig—
Tuned and polished and
Spoken to in secret lingo
And when the weekend was up
And the cover tossed back over
The motorcycle the last look would

Be at the namebadge on the tank which
Read Harley-Davidson and suddenly the
Week that began tomorrow would be tolerated
Because you were a bikerider even when you could not.

JAMES M. GARRIPOLI

Age: Thirty-six
Occupation: Senior Account Representative, 3M Automotive Aftermarket Division
Home: Old Bridge, New Jersey
Years Riding: Twenty-two

I'll start off by telling you who I am. My name is James M. Garripoli; my friends call me Jimmy. I am thirty-six years old. I'm a son, brother, husband, father of two, handyman, salesman and motorcycle enthusiast. I have been riding motorcycles for over twenty-two years, covering many different facets of the sport. I have ridden motocross, raced enduros, toured the United States, navigated through major cities and regularly cruise the back roads of the East.

For me, riding motorcycles has always been more than transportation. It's my time, my escape. Each ride is a unique experience, but never fails to offer a guaranteed thrill. No matter how hectic my life may seem, I always find time to ride, mellow out and regroup. Before I mount my bike (presently it's a 1948 Indian Chief), I carry out a routine mechanical inspection. It gives me a sense of pride to know I perform all of the maintenance on my bikes. After everything checks out, I slip on my leather jacket and boots, tighten up my chaps, adjust my gloves and don my helmet. It almost feels like I am an actor getting into character. At this very moment, I undergo a definite mental transformation.

I begin to clear my head and anticipate the freedom of the ride. It comforts me to know that I am in total control. I take a deep breath, hop on the saddle and spark up the engine. As the bike idles, I study the sweet sound of the exhaust. This always gives me goosebumps; it's been a given from the very first time I ever rode. The smells, sounds and vibrations help me draw all of my attention to the moment. The wife, kids and job are a distant memory and I have not even left the driveway yet! I grind the transmission into gear and disengage the clutch. The ride has begun.

I don't always have a specific destination when I begin a ride. I let the mood of the moment dictate my direction. Do I want to find solace in a desolate back road? Do I want to be an exhibitionist? Do I want the challenge of negotiating hairpin turns through winding back roads? No matter what the discussion, it's all good!

At this point in my life, the rush doesn't come from speed; it comes from the freedom. I enjoy getting glances from a passerby or cruising through a crowd. I love accelerating through a turn on a mountain road or just tooling around the neighborhood. What I am trying to say is that the feeling of what the ride represents is as important as the ride itself. The freedom is my fuel if you will.

When I return home from one of my journeys, I feel exhilarated! Could it be from the wind pounding my face and chest? Or does this feeling come from the clearing of my mind? Am I exhilarated by the physical or mental stimulation? Who cares? The important thing is that I can't wait for my next ride!

WAI "FRANKI" YANG

Age: Fifty-seven
Occupation: Tools, diving equipment and mechanical sales
Home: Hong Kong SAR, China
Years Riding: Forty-one

It was almost Christmas time when I was sitting in front of my computer sending out emails of Seasons Greetings to my correspondents all over the world. When I checked my own mailbox, I noticed there was mail from my Greek biker friend Dimitris, in Hong Kong. He had sent me some brief information about an American guy with an Italian name writing a book about biking and ancient Chinese philosophy. Being one of the organizers of the Global Riders Meeting for the past five years, how global can this get, I thought. My curiosity drove me to ask for more. Emails went back and forth. I found myself committed to write something about my feeling toward motorcycling and how it affected my life. Well, I am not much of a writer; besides, my English is not that good. However, I would like to share my feelings about motorcycle riding with anyone who may be interested or patient enough to try to understand.

I was born in Tsing Tao, Shandong Province, China in 1952. My first experience on a motorcycle was when I was two-and-a-half years old. How can I remember this? Well my beloved father, who is also a biker, took a photo of me sitting on his 500cc BSA. This is the most precious thing I inherited from him, and the same photo got me addicted to vehicles with two wheels. Our family moved to Hong Kong when I was four years old. From primary school to high school, I received a Chinese education in Hong Kong. Being a city where East meets West, I also picked up the English language on the streets, literally. I got my first bicycle when I was ten. Fascinated by the joy of cycling, I rode it to school until I was sixteen. By then, I was tall enough and brave enough to try to ride a motorcycle without a license (the legal age to get a learner's license is eighteen). Newfound freedom on a motorized two-wheeler was so overwhelming that it drove me to invest all my three years hard-earned summer holiday job savings for a 200cc two-stroke Yamaha.

Motorcycle Touring

As time passed, I have grown out of a motorcycle commuter and discovered the joy of touring on a motorcycle. But due to the geographical limitation of Hong Kong, I was only able to go around the territory in "circles." In 1978, I got a job offer to teach scuba diving in the Red Sea. With the spirit of adventure, I went off on a container vessel to Eilat, Israel. For the first time, I discovered a new world so alien to China. The hustle and bustle of a cosmopolitan city like Hong Kong compared to the silence of the cool dark night in the middle of the Sinai Desert, the barrenness of Ras Muhammed and the celebration of marine life underneath the dark blue surface of the Red Sea was eye opening for me. The only thing that related to Asian culture was a dive site named Japanese Garden by the locals. Life was hard, but I did my best to adjust to it. Three months later, with the help of my father, my CB400N arrived in a crate. I began to explore the country and began my lifelong passion of touring on a motorcycle. It strikes a balance in my life, created happiness and inner calm. Soon after that, I toured Europe, where I learned more about Western culture and hospitalities. After returning to Asia, my tours around Southeast Asian countries were almost a yearly getaway from the pressure of work. By 1992, I took a chance by resigning from a well-paying job and started a solo motorcycle tour of North America. Two months and over 10,000 miles later, I returned home with a big smile on my face to carry on with the rat race. Mid-life crisis balanced with a mid-life cruise? Maybe there is some logic to it.

Family

When I first met my wife, the prettiest girl on an island south of Hong Kong, I asked her if she would consider being a pillion passenger on my bike. She joyfully agreed. She has been an excellent pillion on my bike for the past twenty years. Strangely enough, the first thing we looked at when we purchased our new home was the parking area for my motorcycles. Many called us crazy when she was still sitting on the back of my bike carving through canyon road one week before she gave birth to our beloved daughter. There must be some truth to the ancient Chinese saying about teaching to the fetus. Yang Yang, our only daughter, has enjoyed riding with me ever since she was old enough to sit up by herself. She will get her 50cc mini-bike when she turns five years old.

Community

In the late 1980s, I felt the need to share my riding experience and joy with other fellow riders. A group of friends started to meet at regular places every weekend. By 1990, the Motorbike Cruisers Club was officially formed, and it has been my motorcycle family ever since. Being the first non-profit, non-brand–name, non-racing motorcycle club in Hong Kong, we were able to set examples for many other groups to form their own clubs, and catered to the different club cultures. In 1994, I had the fortune to meet the famous Japanese Noh theater percussionist Mr. S. Okura. We shared our views about peace on earth. We then organized the Global Riders Meeting in Japan to bring people of different cultural backgrounds together. Through the common language of music, art and motorcycles, we were able to enjoy and appreciate cultures and friendships from different nations. With that feeling in mind, we returned to Hong Kong and were able to unite most Hong Kong motorcycle traders (they have never been able to share a dinner table since the beginning of their business). We formed the Hong Kong Motorcycle Association to represent motorcyclists as a whole, and to petition and consult with authorities for the better livelihood of the motorcycle trade and the rights of riders. These achievements, though with no material rewards, are very satisfying for me. I can now proudly proclaim that I have lived a full life (so far and hopefully many more years to come), and I am content with what I have done.

Nonbikers

For you nonbikers out there, motorcycle riding means freedom: the wind blowing against your body; the close proximity with nature; the feeling of being in control of a machine and able to negotiate the turns in the road the way you want. Acceleration and centrifugal force are a physical and mechanical joy. With a motorcycle, you can travel to places off the beaten track, meet all kinds of interesting people, and share a common language: motorcycles. It is the same as people who have other hobbies. The bad elements such as motorcycle gangs are just a very small percentage of the biking community, though very well advertised in Hollywood movies. Sure, bikers may be more individualistic, a bit eccentric, but look around at your friends. Aren't they all a bit different? That's what makes life interesting! If I believed in reincarnation, I wouldn't mind being a biker again, or just a plain old motorcycle for that matter.

Global Riders Meeting
Organizer's Introduction

The Global Riders Meeting was formed by the members of the Hiten Percussion Ensemble: Shonosuke Okura, who plays the Noh side drum called Otsuzumi; Kim Dae Hwan, Korean percussionist; and Franki Yang from the Motorbike Cruisers Club (MCC) (Hong Kong). The first Global Riders Meeting was held in 1994 with motorcycle riders from several countries attending.

The fiftieth anniversary of the end of WWII was marked in 1995. Twenty-eight members from MCC started the first leg of the tour, with sixteen remaining for the whole eighteen-day trip. Some members got an OBE (out-of-body experience), while others found friendship, understanding of a different culture and had a great time in general. Many riders from North America, Europe and Asia also attended this great event with multimedia (TV, newspapers, magazines, video production, etc.) coverage throughout Japan. Magazines and newspapers in Hong Kong, Macao and Korea also reported this event.

For the organization, 1997 was the year of Back to Nature. We toured Shikoku Island, the least-developed main island of Japan. We travelled by boat (Sunflower Line) with our bikes from Tokyo, and toured by bike throughout Shikoku. We swept the mountain twisties, slept in shrines and temples, swam in the beautiful Shimanju River, and sang by the campfire at the stony riverbed. Old acquaintances were renewed and new friends made. Many friends shared their tears when we had to say good-bye. It was another wonderful experience of a lifetime.

In 1998, the fifth anniversary of GRM was celebrated. We toured the Hokkaido Island, the northern main island which was a biker's paradise. The reality was, most nights were spent at campsites with toilet facilities provided. It was a whole new experience for city dwellers like us, but it was hard. We experienced lots of nature, scenic spots, hot springs, fishing harbors, mouth-watering seafood and delicious local restaurants, and very warm hospitality. Extra bonuses were the magnificent scenery of natural Hokkaido. We experienced the beautiful native people, Ainu, and mixed with top performing artists from many countries. As usual, Global Riders Meeting is not a deluxe organized tour on two wheels. It is a mission on two wheels. The spirit is to spread the word of peace and, during the process, to gain an understanding of different cultures and different strokes. Hopefully we can live with others and ourselves in peace.

The price of each trip was on a cost-sharing basis. You had to pay for the return airfare to Narita, Tokyo, all hotel accommodations while staying in the Tokyo area, club management fee, fuel, insurance, GRM joining fee, highway toll, breakfast and some other meals during the trip when we were unable to meet according to our scheduled itinerary, and personal expenses. Bikes were supplied free of charge from sponsors, but responsibility for all liabilities and damages rested on the individual who was riding the bike. You were also expected to take turns driving a backup car/van. An international driving license valid for Japan was a must.

Most meals and accommodations during the ride were provided. You had to bring a sleeping bag for cool nights. Protective riding gear—i.e., helmet, gloves, boots—was compulsory. Other protective riding gear and wet weather gear was highly recommended.

Contact:
Motorbike Cruisers Club / Franki Yang
Kowloon, Hong Kong
Tel: (852) 2338-6337
Fax: (852) 2336-7640
Email: *yansermc@netfront.net*

DR. HORST MICHAEL "DOC MIKE" BIRKHOFF

Age: Thirty-eight
Occupation: Dentist
Home: Dusseldorf, West Germany
Years Riding: Twenty-two

Motorcycling kind of takes me back to my roots. When I was a sixteen-year-old boy, I got my first motorcycle. It was a small 50cc Kreidler, but I went on a two thousand-mile trip through Germany, Netherlands, Belgium, France and Luxembourg. Even visited Paris with it! Since I was raised in a small town, this small 50cc hummer enlarged my world: For the first time in my life I could go wherever I wanted— I was free!!! Even today, more than twenty years later, I still remember that first ride out of my hometown, with the sun in both mirrors! And I still get that feeling of freedom, and everyday sorrows just disappear with every beat of the big V-Twin under my butt. Interestingly, Harleys seem to work best with that kind of "biker philosophy." I have ridden all kinds of bikes and liked most of them, but there's nothing compared to my Harley. Don't know why; maybe the rumble of that V-Twin is kind of synchronized to a human heartbeat? Hell, who knows—doesn't matter anyway; it's just pure plain fun. Feeling good! It clears my head and soul! And for me, it's the key to meeting interesting people who live and feel like me. Not everyone on a bike is a good person. But it still is the platform to meet the best friends you'll ever have.

AMY HOLLAND

Age: Thirty-four
Occupation: California Motorcycle Safety
Instructor
Home: Somis, California
Years Riding: Seventeen

Words cannot describe my feelings while riding a motor-bike. Yeah, it's all about the freedom of the open road, the wind in your face, the "destination unknown" feeling that motorcycling brings. But it's also deeper than that. It's becoming one with myself and thinking about absolutely nothing that keeps me from feeling centered. Who can think about their bad day at work or the fight they had with their spouse when flying along the road, at one with the elements and the sound of the engine beneath you?

Riding a motorcycle forces me to think about the here and now, rather than about what lies ahead. Whatever I do while riding directly affects my future, but I can't really think about the future because I don't want to make a mistake now. What is happening *right now* is all that really matters; the future will get here when it gets here.

The oddest thing happened to me the other day. My commute to work is an hour or an hour and fifteen minutes; I've been doing this ride for about a month and a half now. When I got to work on Monday, I parked the bike, locked it up, picked up my tank bag and headed into the building. I have to walk down a very long hall before I reach my office. I was halfway down the hall before I slowly realized where I was. I had been so absorbed with the ride that I completely forgot where I was going. It was just one of those days where I could have ridden forever.

Riding a motorcycle takes me completely away from the mundane side of life. It doesn't matter if I'm commuting through heavy L.A. traffic, riding from Burns to Bend Oregon, or riding through the Mojave Desert after a trip to Las Vegas. Whatever bike I'm riding becomes an extension of myself; I personify the motorbike into a living, breathing being. Instead of just me travelling along the road, it becomes "us." We encounter bad weather, crazy traffic or heavenly twisty roads. I am never alone. My best friend is always right there beneath me, through good and bad, for better or for worse. We journey through life together.

The process of riding a motorcycle has made me realize that my destiny lies totally within myself. Outside influences are to be dealt with, surmounted, then forgotten. If anything happens, it is my own fault and I have no one to blame but myself. Hopefully, my mistake is not costly—I learn from it and move on. Same with my daily life: I am responsible for myself and my actions. If I want to achieve a particular goal, it is up to me and me alone to see that it gets done. I must make my presence known if I expect to survive, but I must not be obnoxious.

Motorcycling is an intensely personal activity; no two riders see a road the same way. I get the most pleasure out of a ride when the road has only two lanes and plenty of wide sweeping turns. Out in the country or through the pungent smell of pine trees—it makes no difference to me. There's just something sweet about a blurred yellow line passing through my peripheral vision, as I make a smooth uphill left-hand sweeper. I found that road while riding towards the north rim of the Grand Canyon; I would make that trip again just to experience the same curve, the same feeling of peace I had while riding through that curve.

Why don't I feel the same while driving a car? A car has way too much insulation. I can't hear the birds, the engine; I can't smell the fragrances that are so abundant when I'm riding a motorcycle. Most of my body goes into a sleep state while driving a car; on my motorcycle, every part of me feels alive—especially my brain. I am processing information, controlling my hands and feet, and absorbing sounds, smells and sights that tell me I am alive and that I am an active participant in my life.

HERBERT DASILVA

Age: Forty
Occupation: 4x4 and industrial vehicle sales
Home: Casuarina, Australia
Years Riding: Thirty

I was born in Rio de Janeiro, Brazil. I came to Australia with my parents in 1974. My love for the Harley-Davidson motorcycle started way before my teenage years. I loved the sound they made, and that is what started it all. I remember the military police bikes then, and they were great. So after many years and immigrating to Down Under, many of my dreams and goals came true. I joined the Australian army in 1980 (1st commando regiment) and not long after that, the Harley-Davidson came up again. I finally bought my first bike and it was a soul-lifting experience. All I can say is that riding is the best way for me to relax and tune up with the surroundings. Up to date, I have rode many, many miles on different rides and now I have my whole family involved. I am the editor of the Darwin Harley-Davidson Owners Group (HOG) chapter and my wife is the secretary. My wife also enjoys the rides as well as my six-year-old daughter who is a great ambassador for Harley. Riding with a group of friends or on my own, I always enjoy that great feeling and excitement on each ride. The looks you get when you arrive at some pubs or while stopped at traffic lights are great. People notice the sound and the smile on your face. Sometimes just riding nowhere in particular I feel as if the bike and myself are one. For some reason I find myself a lot calmer and more relaxed after a long ride. I guess the joy and great feeling that you share with other riders makes up for the often long and tiring rides. I always tell people that no two Harleys are the same. Each Harley is personal and unique to each rider. I can only say that riding is so much part of my life now that I can't imagine not being able to ride.

LARRY MARROTTE

Age: Fifty
Occupation: Structural engineer, weight trainer
Home: Mililani, Oahu, Hawaii
Years Riding: Thirty-one

What is a biker?

I hear this all the time. Some people look at you like you are some nut on two wheels, and others look at you and wish they had the guts to try it.

I was asked to put pen to paper on what it is that makes you want to get on a motorcycle. First, for the non-riders, you know that there's the so-called "want to be biker" out there, we call them (wannabes). You know, the guys on HDs with fake tattoos and rugs on their bean bag heads, acting bad to the bone, weekend warriors; and then they're Mr. GQ the rest of the week. Just because you ride a motorcycle doesn't make you a biker. A biker is a person who sleeps, eats, reads and rides in his or her heart on the back of a bike or in front. My friend, an old lady, rides in the winter and summer, in seventeen-and-a-half hours of rain, storm, heat in the desert, freezing mountain passes, and does not complain one time about it. She knows more about bikes than your average biker. She's a biker!

My wife is and will always be a biker. I remember the first time my girlfriend, now my wife, got on the back of a motorcycle. I asked my friend if I could use his bike, a 350 Honda, to go from Newark, New Jersey to Allentown, Pennsylvania. She did not say anything or complain. At that point I knew she was the one. After we got together and I sold my bike, she looked at me, at the house we were in, and the kids, and asked me to take her to the bike shop to look at some bikes. I did not know at the time that she had picked out a new bike for us—a new 1980 KZ1300B2 Kawasaki—and got a job to pay for it. We still have that bike. I have sold my other bikes—an R/60 BMW, KZ1000, FLH, XLCH, GRZ and a CBR1000. I had all the major brands—over four hundred and fifty bikes, yes, four hundred and fifty bikes, and the guys who know me will back me up on this one.

I own my own bike shop now. I meet all types of bikers, outlaw biker MC [*motorcycle clubs—G.G.*] and MG [*motorcycle gangs—G.G.*] on their rags—the "1 percent" we call them. These dudes are street tough guys—from 'Nam Vets to plain old hard core. Then there are the free and sober clubs, Black clubs and Black outlaws, all-girl clubs, Christian riding clubs, cop clubs, firefighter MC, Latin MC, fag MC, three-wheel clubs. As much as they would like to be new or different, when it all comes down to money or toy runs for the kids, everybody just gives it up. The "1 percent"—the "Bad Boys" of biking—will give more money to kids' runs than any other group. They, more than anybody, will go the long haul for the kids' blood runs or cancer runs. This part of biking is not known to John Q. Public. You don't read about this, and they would like to keep it that way.

I saw this guy on a Honda scooter with a roof on top and a can body on the bottom at a ton of gatherings—Daytona

Beach Bike Americade; Lake George, New York; Sturgis, South Dakota; Rolling Thunder, New York City and D.C.— to the wall. To me this guy is a biker! He qualified as a biker—no fake rug, no fake tattoos. He lay what he got up front as a biker.

I have seen the good side and the bad side. My first ride was on a Vespa motor scooter in the pineapple fields of Hawaii. It was all uphill or down. I've since ridden all over the lower forty-eight, plus Hawaii, Puerto Rico, Canada, Mexico and overseas throughout Europe. But the best time for me was when me and my son took our first ride from Newark, New Jersey to Front Royal, Virginia, then to Asheville, North Carolina. We camped out and spent time together, met other bikers on the Skyline Drive and the Blue Ridge Parkway. We stopped and looked out over the mountains as the sun was coming up and saw a bald eagle soaring overhead. We stopped to hear some guys playing the banjo and guitar-picking, and just jamming by themselves. We camped and talked to people with Southern accents—this my son heard for the first time. He looked at me and said these people talked funny and asked me where they were from. I told him that they spoke with this accent and came from South Carolina, and people from the southern states have what we call a southern drawl and, if anything, we sound funny to them. We had a great time just riding and camping out. Now when we get together we talk about that trip we took back then and how we'd like to do it one more time. He has his own rugrat now. I hope he takes him on his first ride, too—just like we did.

P.S. I think I will put the bug in his son's ear—maybe he will take me, too!

READER/CUSTOMER CARE SURVEY

If you are enjoying this book, please help us serve you better and meet your changing needs by taking a few minutes to complete this survey. Please fold it & drop it in the mail.

As a special **"Thank You"** we'll send you news about interesting books and a valuable **Gift Certificate.**

PLEASE PRINT

NAME: _____

ADDRESS: _____

_____

TELEPHONE NUMBER: _____

FAX NUMBER: _____

E-MAIL: _____

WEBSITE: _____

(1) Gender: 1)_____Female 2)_____Male

(2) Age:
1)_____12 or under   5)_____30-39
2)_____13-15   6)_____40-49
3)_____16-19   7)_____50-59
4)_____20-29   8)_____60+

(3) Your Children's Age(s):
Check all that apply.
1)_____6 or Under   3)_____11-14
2)_____7-10   4)_____15-18

(7) Marital Status:
1)_____Married
2)_____Single
3)_____Divorced/Wid.

(8) Was this book
1)_____Purchased for yourself?
2)_____Received as a gift?

(9) How many Chicken Soup books have you bought or read?
1)_____1   3)_____3
2)_____2   4)_____4+

(10) How did you find out about this book?
Please check ONE.
1)_____Personal Recommendation
2)_____Store Display
3)_____TV/Radio Program
4)_____Bestseller List
5)_____Website
6)_____Advertisement/Article or Book Review
7)_____Catalog or mailing
8)_____Other_____

(11) What FIVE subject areas do you enjoy reading about most?
Rank: 1 (favorite) through 5 (least favorite)
A)_____ Self Development
B)_____ New Age/Alternative Healing
C)_____ Storytelling
D)_____ Spirituality/Inspiration
E)_____ Family and Relationships
F)_____ Health and Nutrition
G)_____ Recovery
H)_____ Business/Professional
I) _____ Entertainment
J) _____ Teen Issues
K)_____ Pets

(16) Where do you purchase most of your books?
Check the top TWO locations.
A)_____ General Bookstore
B)_____ Religious Bookstore
C)_____ Warehouse/Price Club
D)_____ Discount or Other Retail Store
E)_____ Website
F)_____ Book Club/Mail Order

(18) Did you enjoy the stories in this book?
1)_____Almost All
2)_____Few
3)_____Some

(19) What type of magazine do you SUBSCRIBE to?
Check up to FIVE subscription categories.
A)_____ General Inspiration
B)_____ Religious/Devotional
C)_____ Business/Professional
D)_____ World News/Current Events
E)_____ Entertainment
F)_____ Homemaking, Cooking, Crafts
G)_____ Women's Issues
H)_____ Other (please specify) _____

(24) Please indicate your income level
1)_____Student/Retired-fixed income
2)_____Under $25,000
3)_____$25,000-$50,000
4)_____$50,001-$75,000
5)_____$75,001-$100,000
6)_____Over $100,000

Additional comments you would like to make:

(31) Are you:
1) A Parent? _____
2) A Grandparent? _____

The Life Issues Publisher

Thank You!!
HCI

(26) If you answered yes, what type?
Check all that apply.
1) _____ Business/Financial
2) _____ Motivational
3) _____ Religious/Spiritual
4) _____ Job-related
5) _____ Family/Relationship issues

(25) Do you attend seminars?
1) _____ Yes   2) _____ No

FOLD HERE

BUSINESS REPLY MAIL
FIRST-CLASS MAIL PERMIT NO 45 DEERFIELD BEACH, FL

POSTAGE WILL BE PAID BY ADDRESSEE

HEALTH COMMUNICATIONS, INC.
3201 SW 15TH STREET
DEERFIELD BEACH, FL 33442-9875

ELAINE C. WHITE

Age:	Forty-six
Occupation:	Publisher and craft book editor
Home:	Sturgis, Missouri
Years Riding:	Thirty-one

I'm a forty-six-year-old female who learned to ride a motorcycle at age fifteen. My father simply presented me with a Honda 90 and said, "See if you can ride this thing." The centrifugal clutch enabled me to learn quickly, and soon I was putting all over the countryside. Often, I was barefoot and always rode without a helmet. I got a kick out of being the only girl in town who owned a motorcycle.

One summer day, I wore shorts and rode my Honda down the main street of my small hometown. I noticed another teenager traveling toward me. He was also on a motorcycle. It was John, a friend of mine from school. He recognized me as well and swerved to the centerline and rode toward me. I also swerved to the centerline and continued toward him. I wondered when he would pull back into a safe path of travel and decided that I wouldn't move at all. We collided head-on.

Upon impact, time was like a slow-motion movie. There was plenty of time to think as I felt my body fly through the air. I remember some of the thoughts: "I'm going to be dead when I hit the ground." "My dad will be sorry he gave me this motorcycle." "My mother will cry for years." "I'll miss seeing the world."

I landed on the pavement, which was sprinkled with gravel, and time was again like a slow-motion movie. More thoughts: "I'm going to slam into something and splatter myself all over the place." "I'll be an ugly sight for someone to see." "My butt is being ground to hamburger." "Seems like I'm sliding a long time." "I'll try to get up."

I put my feet on the ground and pressed as I tried to stand. I stopped sliding and began tumbling. My head banged the pavement. I realized that I was motionless, but alive. I raised my head to look toward my father's service station that was nearby. In the center of my vision was a black, blurry spot. The most frightening thought of all screamed through my brain—"I'm blind!"

Time was no longer like a slow-motion movie. It was like a movie at double-speed. Thoughts shot through my mind so quickly that within seconds, I imagined a hundred scenarios about life as a blind person—all the way to old age, and I didn't like what I saw. I heard a loud wailing and realized it was my own voice crying to the gods. It was not a scream of pain as the onlookers probably thought. It was a scream of anguish over my lost eyesight.

At fifteen I learned firsthand about hysterical blindness, which is only a temporary loss of eyesight. My physical injuries were slight compared to the emotional upset the accident caused. My motorcycle was a total wreck. Secretly, I was glad it couldn't be repaired.

Thirty years later, I was divorced when I met Vech, an expert on antique BMW motorcycles. Our courtship included many discussions about his love of riding and working on antique bikes. Over a period of several months I realized the desire to ride was blossoming inside me. I remembered the wind, freedom and thrill I felt when I was fifteen while riding my motorcycle. I wanted that feeling again. I wanted to ride again, not just any motorcycle, but an antique motorcycle.

Although I had riding experience, it took a while to grow accustomed to the 1968 500cc BMW Vech and I restored. The first time I rode it, I admit I was scared. I shook, my stomach hurt and I thought I was going to vomit. Yeah, it was that bad. The thing is, my desire to ride helped overcome my physical and psychological discomfort. A good instructor helped, too. My instructor was patient and didn't push me at all. Somehow all my apprehension was related to letting go of the clutch for the first time. I hesitated about two dozen times before I felt the motorcycle lurch to life. My fear reached its peak, but I didn't freeze (maybe determination to keep the thing upright and going helped here too). I was off to a wobbly start.

As I increased speed, the motorcycle was much easier to handle. I made a slow, gradual turn and guess what? I had that old feeling again—the feeling of riding again! It was all psychologically and physically draining. I stopped smoothly and took a few minutes to catch my breath and let what just happened sink in. I needed to relax a bit before I was ready to try again, and guess what? That old fear of letting out the clutch hit me all over again. It was hard, but it didn't take as long as the first time before I was brave enough to let it out again. Over and over I started and stopped, getting the feel of the clutch and the amount of motorcycle I had under me. (The last time I rode, it was a 90cc and under me now was a 500cc.)

Now (one year later), I am very proud of my beautiful antique motorcycle, and I ride it as often as possible. Riding a motorcycle requires concentrating on my surroundings. I spot traffic and try to imagine what could happen that would cause an accident. I do this so that I can prepare mentally for what may come. It sounds as if I'm "riding in fear," but it's not really that way at all. Fear isn't the motivator. I choose to think it's smart preparation . . . preparation and concentration that could save my life.

When I ride I become exhilarated. The adrenaline soars as I feel the power beneath me. Sometimes, I can be at peace with the world on my motorcycle when a cruel thought invades my pleasure—"It could happen now."

"It" means another accident. I realize "It" is my own doubt caused by negative thinking. "It" spoils my pleasure. I quickly push "It" out of my mind so that I may concentrate on my surroundings and the motorcycle beneath me. Mental balance allows me to enjoy the ride. Without a positive outlook, fear invades. In turn, the fear steals my concentration. Without concentration, I know I'm in danger of having another accident. Without concentration, I can have no pleasure.

It takes strong mental discipline in order for me to concentrate and enjoy the ride. At the end of each ride, I celebrate my victory over fear and negative thinking. I feel awe at the power of my mind and the forces that allow me to control "It" rather than "It" control me. I feel more confident, powerful and ready to accept new challenges. I know that I can do anything I allow my mind to imagine.

GIANNI NAPOLITANO

Age: Twenty-two
Occupation: Student
Home: Positano, Basilicato, Italy
Years Riding: One

I've had my Motoguzzi for one year now, and I love it. We always rode motopeds when we were young. The petrol here is so expensive and there aren't many families that have cars anyway. We have one Fiat for three families in my hometown. Everything is so close, it is always easier to walk than find a parking space. What is there to see outside of town anyway?

Then I went to university last year in Rome, and the whole world opened up. I got my Motoguzzi, I moved to Rome, and everything changed so fast. The motorcycle is like a symbol of all this to me. I get on my bike and cruise on the Appian Way, and it makes me feel like I am drunk. This is our ancient highway from the great Roman Empire; it's over two thousand years old. It makes me crazy to ride a new motorcycle on a road that was once filled with chariots.

When I need a break from classes, there is always a girl from school who wants to jump on the back of my bike and enjoy a ride. This is good. You know, a woman who likes the motorcycle, she's a good woman. She is not scared of anything. We like to go up to the mountains near the Papa's

[*Pope's*—G.G.] summer home. The roads are so windy, the girls hold on so tight. There is one stretch of road where you always stop your bike. It looks like the road is going downhill, but when you lift your feet, you start rolling backwards! It's a crazy trick of the eyes, like so many things in life. The women love it!

But the Motoguzzi, she is real, no tricks. Like a woman herself, she teaches me many things when we ride . . . and she gives me many pleasures. After a long cruise in the country, I come back to the university in the city and feel like a new man. What a great gift such an engine on two wheels is!

CARL JOHNSON

Age: Forty-two
Occupation: Grocer
Home: San Rafael, California
Years Riding: Twenty

Motorcycling is a suspended state of time and reality in which I can let my head clear of all unwanted thoughts. There is a clearer understanding of things important such as family, friends, self and keeping this mass of chrome, horsepower and flesh on the road.

As I fly down roads, familiar scenes of countryside pass in the chrome reflections. I momentarily get lost in the vision of the world passing by into a chromium vortex that is my headlamp. Just as quick I'm back at seventy miles per hour coming up quick on a slow cage [car] rolling down the road. And so it goes, mile after wondrous mile of planet Earth under my wheels.

I've been riding Harleys since 1981 so the new millenium will be my twentieth year. I enjoy the ride, the scenery and the camaraderie of the whole motorcycling experience. We have a small group (about 150) of bikers that also do charity drives and social events. We're known as the Rip City Riders. It's a loose-knit group of friends that includes jewelers, grocers, rock stars and carpenters . . . and more. At forty-two years of age, I appreciate life itself more from my motorcycling days and the good times, good friends and peace of mind on Earth it gives me. I've made many wonderful friendships through my life and many more to come I know will follow.

Here are some of my "favorites" in life:

Favorite motorcycling song:
   "Born to Be Wild"
Favorite ride:
   Redwood Run (San Francisco to Garberville, California)
Favorite people:
   My wife and son

Thanx. Ride safe.

RUSS ALBUMS

Age:	Fifty
Occupation:	Radio Personality
Home:	Tampa, Florida
Years Riding:	Thirty-eight

To some, riding is a way of life . . . to some, an escape . . . to some, a thrill . . . to some, freedom. Since my ride began at twelve, it has embraced all of the above, and in those thirty-eight years it has even added a new feeling. Flight. The wind assumes that Mach 5 sound, enhanced by its feel. The aura of the complete uninhibited field of vision a hawk must experience. Unencumbered by windshields and door-posts, or a roof, you can escape within the sound of your throbbing twin, and through the ungated presence of mind, be in a field of silence. Your complete control of its control as you become one with your machine is liberating! The escape, whether it's from a job, a circumstance or person, can be fulfilling on its own, or can be shared. Each circum-stance has a feeling of its own. The thrill of flight, the feel-ing and sound of power are pure exhilaration. Life takes a new start every time you saddle-up. Every revolution of your V-Twin is waiting for you to take complete control and begin another foray into your own personal wild blue yonder, whether it's the peaceful, flowing wings of a dove or the untrapped wings of Mercury's fleet journeys. You alone are in command of your daily destiny when you get a grip on the throttle and taxi down your driveway. Have a great flight!!

BRENDA JOY LEM

Age: Thirty-seven
Occupation: Artist and political/community activist
Home: Toronto, Ontario, Canada
Years Riding: As a passenger, seven; solo for three

"Yahn bao het"

"When you drive a car 'het bao yahn' or 'the metal wraps around the person,' protecting him or her. When you drive a motorcycle 'yahn bao het'; it is the person wrapping around, protecting the metal." My cousin warns me of the danger or, in her opinion, the apparent lunacy of riding a motorcycle.

The first time I saw my motorcycle, I have to say I felt intimidated by the beast—by its size, its power, by its sheer beauty. The first time I rode her, I felt fear, fear of dropping and possibly damaging her. I am ninety-five pounds and my 450cc Honda Nighthawk weighed in around 450 pounds so unlike a lot of men, I could not muscle the beast to control it. I felt a challenge to learn to work with her power. From Tai Chi and Kung fu, I knew I had to learn to use what little weight I had to most advantage. I understood I needed to use the strength of my challenger to my own advantage and to focus what little strength I had at the appropriate moments. I have often applied this philosophy when dealing with the painful experiences of racism. Learning to stay calm in the face of outright hatred or just plain belittlement due to stereotypes of Asian woman and finding the right moment to throw my opponent off balance with a well-placed remark. As someone who is very cerebral, the motorcycle offers me an opportunity to apply this philosophy in a very direct physical sense.

To ride my motorcycle was to practice this art. As one is a "practicing" Buddhist, or a practicing artist, I was a practicing motorcyclist. I regret to admit that I did drop her a few times when she was at a standstill. I remember the anxiety as I pulled up to a red light. I was not tall enough to place my feet fully on the ground, just the balls of my feet, and my legs would be shaking. With the passing of time, I slowly gained confidence and developed greater awareness of my relationship to "Bunny." She looked like a rabbit when she had her cover on. I was learning to ride her with concentration and discipline of both my mind and my body. Eventually, I was able to ride her on camping trips and a trip from Toronto to Ottawa.

There is no better way to go on a camping trip than on a motorcycle. If your goal is to be outdoors and aware of nature as it surrounds you, then to be on a motorcycle means you are outdoors from the moment you leave your house to the moment you return. I can recall getting up at dawn and pulling out in the damp gray chill of a fall morning to see a gopher munching on greens along the side of the road and a hawk soaring overhead. In a car, I would have been warm, insulated, "het bao yahn." But through that band of windshield, I would not have been even aware of the hawk soaring over the roof of the car or of the gopher.

In a wealthy country like Canada, we are too often insulated in our warm comfortable houses and cars. With such comforts, it is easy to lose awareness of what surrounds us in nature and how we impact on the environment. Particularly in urban environments, we may no longer even be in direct contact with plants, the soil or undomesticated animals. And in that insular world, it is very easy to ignore or be blind to what is happening to those who are less fortunate than us. To shed the protection of "het bao yahn" can help us develop a greater mindfulness both on the motorcycle and off.

The motorcycle is not designed for the city. It does not like to be constantly stop and go, or to be stationary. It is meant to move. And like Tai Chi, when that energy is being expended, it can be more easily managed. The motorcycle longs to be moving on the open road, or cutting through forests and mountain passes. As one riding a motorcycle, I have learned that I need to feel that energy and to use the path of least resistance to keep the energy flowing.

In life, we often meet something that intimidates us and causes us fear. If we can learn to respect it and to use it for our own advantage then we have learned a very useful skill.

TIM SPERO

Age:	Thirty-nine
Occupation:	Sound Designer, Partner, West End Recording
Home:	Tampa, Florida
Years Riding:	Twenty-five

LIKE FATHER , LIKE . . .
IN LOVING MEMORY OF RALPH J. DADY II

I received my first motorcycle, from my stepfather, as a gift for my fourteenth birthday in 1973. The bike was a 125cc Harley-Davidson that I believe was made in Italy by Aramacchi. While my friends were in the "field" at the end of our street riding their Honda 50s and 90s I was already labeled the "outlaw" on the Harley. There was nowhere in my hometown of Waukegan, Illinois (the "s" is silent) that I could not get to either legally or otherwise even though I did not have a driver's license.

At this time, I must point out that my dad never owned a Harley. He had a Honda 750, several Goldwings, including the first model year, two Kawasaki Z-1 900cc motorcycles and sometime in the early 1970s he discovered BMW. Soon after buying his first R90, I noticed that his interest in all other motorcycles waned. A sidecar would turn up in the garage only to disappear with the bike it was attached to. Days later, they would magically reappear in full dress with a custom paint job (he always stayed with those horrid shades of BMW orange and purple). One of his bikes even won first prize for best dresser at a BMWMOA rally.

Soon after I turned sixteen, I moved up to the world of the full-fledged outlaw and acquired a Sportster. On any given summer Saturday, my dad and I would walk out to the garage and prepare to go for a ride. Most times he would end up leaving by himself while I tried to figure out why the Sportster wouldn't start. Occasionally, in a gesture of family solidarity, I jumped in the sidecar and joined him on a romp through southeast Wisconsin, dangerously close to the hallowed city of Milwaukee. I have fond memories of hanging on for dear life when we turned because dad was about six feet, five inches and three hundred pounds. I remember pulling over at roadhouses all over northern Illinois and southern Wisconsin and being introduced as "my son Tim." This always made me feel so proud not to be referred to as a "stepson" and I also got a kick out of the number of people who stated that they could see the resemblance (this only happened when I wasn't riding the Harley).

Over the years, I went through a number of Harleys including a Sprint 350 made by Aramacchi in Italy. I moved to Florida in 1979 after spending a year ski bumming in Utah. My dad encouraged me to take the time to travel around while I was young because I would be stuck in some career I didn't like with a mortgage and credit card debt soon enough. He practiced law and was quite good at it when he was not holding court in the bar at the Collins-Karcher Hotel or another of his favorite haunts.

While I lived in Clearwater, Florida in 1980 and 1981, I laid my bike down on two separate occasions in a short period of time. After the second crash, I decided that my lifestyle clashed with the average age of the Clearwater driver (eighty-two years) and I sold what was left of my bike and did not ride for ten years. Dad went through some bad times in the 1980s. After giving up on the law and selling his bikes, he bought a campground in Kentucky. He went through another divorce (number six) and lost the campground. He disappeared for a while, and when he turned up things were not good. He died in a VA hospital in Nashville in 1991. [While writing this, I called my mother to find out the year of their divorce (1970), and I realized that, when the events of this story took place, he was not even my stepfather but just a guy who took an active interest in helping to raise the son of his third (ex)wife. Perhaps one of his more responsible acts.]

After my father's death, I decided that I had matured enough to maneuver a bike among the "blue hairs." After looking at the new Harleys, I decided I had neither the money nor the patience to purchase a new one. I was equally disappointed to find that thanks to the popularity of "posing" by a Harley, used ones were out of my reach as well. Then I spotted an ad in the Cycle Trader for a 1981 BMW R-65. The price was right, and a short time later I realized I had become my father.

I now have a 1995 R-100 Mystic, no orange or purple for me. In the past I would take a ride at least every weekend and I would always think about the man who gave me my first bike. These days I don't ride as much because I spend 99 percent of my free time with my two-year-old son, Dylan. He likes to sit on my Beemer and make engine sounds. Now that he talks, he tells me he wants to go for a ride. I explain to him that we will spend plenty of time riding when he is old enough, and I look forward to the day when we can hit the road and I can tell him stories about the grandfather he never knew.

JED FARMER

Age: Seventy-four
Home: Memphis, Tennessee
Occupation: Mechanic
Years Riding: Fifty-one

I don't have a lot of fancy words to say about riding. Riding is just riding. It's like life; life is just for living. All the extra stuff you say about it is really just the bullshit that keeps you from living. We all need reminders from time to time, I imagine. I find myself thinking about some of the wildest stuff when I'm on a long ride. Thoughts about how everything in life is really simple once you just let go. I used to fight a lot when I was young; that's just the way it was back then. We were just kids when we were sent over to Normandy in World War II . . . that was real fighting. Coming back home in one piece made me think twice about what it meant to be alive. I got a lot more level-headed and started to appreciate the basic things in life. Like riding a motorcycle.

When I returned from duty, some rich kid in town just got a brand-spanking new '48 Indian Chief and didn't know shit about riding. Well, neither did I but at least I kick-started that puppy and took it for a spin. That kid liked to sit on it while it was idling, making believe I think. It's like a lot of these young turks you see on bikes these days. Their darn bikes look so clean; you know they never even ride 'em in the rain. What good is doing something if it's all for show?

Who you trying to impress anyway? If it's not for your heart, it's just showing off, and you only waste everybody's time. I used to go down dirt roads back home and cake that new bike up with so much mud you couldn't even find that great little Indian chief's head anywhere on it. I'd be so happy. The kid never did take it out for so much as a ride to the gas pump. But that's the way his whole life was I suppose. He ended up giving me that old bike for a birthday gift . . . bless his heart.

I wish I had it when I went to Sturgis [*a massive annual Harley gathering in South Dakota—G. G.*] this year. I took my trusty Road King. That bike makes me dream of my old '58 Duo Glide. I love these rallies. People say I'm getting too old to ride but I tell 'em to stick it. As long as I can walk, I can ride. I've been through too much in my life to quit doing what I enjoy. If I learned one thing, it's that the more you do what you enjoy, the longer and happier you're gonna live doing it. My wife still loves to get on the back of our Harley and go for rides. What the hell, why quit a good thing when it's still good? And when I can't ride no more, I've memories enough for both of us.

Ride safe.

Permissions *(continued from page ii)*

Material contributed by Dr. Horst Michael "Doc Mike" Birkhoff reprinted by permission of Dr. Horst Michael "Doc Mike" Birkhoff. ©1999 Dr. Horst Michael "Doc Mike" Birkhoff.

Material contributed by Amy Holland reprinted by permission of Amy Holland. ©1999 Amy Holland.

Material contributed by Herbert Dasilva reprinted by permission of Herbert Dasilva. ©1999 Herbert Dasilva.

Material contributed by Larry Marrotte reprinted by permission of Larry Marrotte. ©1999 Larry Marrotte.

Material contributed by Elaine C. White reprinted by permission of Elaine C. White. ©1999 Elaine C. White.

Material contributed by Gianni Napolitano reprinted by permission of Gianni Napolitano. ©1999 Gianni Napolitano.

Material contributed by Carl Johnson reprinted by permission of Carl Johnson. ©1999 Carl Johnson.

Material contributed by Russ Albums reprinted by permission of Russ Albums. ©1999 Russ Albums.

Material contributed by Brenda Joy Lem reprinted by permission of Brenda Joy Lem. ©1999 Brenda Joy Lem.

Material contributed by Tim Spero reprinted by permission of Tim Spero. ©1999 Tim Spero.

Material contributed by Jed Farmer reprinted by permission of Jed Farmer. ©1999 Jed Farmer.

ABOUT THE AUTHOR

Garri Garripoli, longtime Harley-Davidson enthusiast and director/producer of the public television documentary *Qigong: Ancient Chinese Healing for the 21st Century*, has practiced Qigong and Eastern healing arts for over twenty years. He left a full scholarship in premed at the University of Colorado during the mid-1970s to study with a renowned master of Eastern healing in Hawaii.

His varied work for public television earned him an Emmy Award and reflects his passionate studies in Traditional Chinese Medicine and alternative healing modalities. He has traveled extensively throughout China and Tibet, writing books, television and film scripts, as well as articles for martial arts magazines.

He is also the author of *Qigong: Essence of the Healing Dance* (Health Communications, Inc., 1999).

Please visit his Web site: *www.WujiProductions.com*

Also from Garri Garripoli

Qigong: Essence of the Healing Dance

"To live in harmony as a civilization, as a nation, as a community or as a couple, we must first live in harmony as a self. This is our ultimate responsibility if we wish to live to our full potential."
— *Garri Garripoli*

You carry within yourself the ability to heal. Learn to tap into this innate gift and dance your own dance of life. You are sure to find this book fascinating, even life changing. A must-read for anyone intrigued by the mystique of ancient Eastern healing arts or seeking a daily practice that promotes and maintains full-body well-being.

Code #6749 Paperback - $12.95

Chicken Soup for the Couple's Soul

Whether single, married or separated, everyone wants to find and keep this elusive thing called "love." Bestselling author and foremost relationship expert Barbara De Angelis teams up as a co-author of *Chicken Soup for the Couple's Soul,* a collection of heartwarming stories about how real people discovered true love with the person of their dreams. A sweet spoonful of this enchanting Chicken Soup collection will warm the hearts of romantic readers everywhere.

Code #6463 Paperback • $12.95

New Chicken Soup for the Soul

Chicken Soup for the Golfer's Soul

This inspiring collection of stories from professionals, caddies and amateur golfers shares the memorable moments of the game—when, despite all odds, an impossible shot lands in the perfect position; when a simple game of golf becomes a lesson in life. Chapters include: sportsmanship, family, overcoming obstacles, perfecting the game and the nineteenth hole. This is a great read for any golfer, no matter what their handicap.

Code #6587 • $12.95

A 6th Bowl of Chicken Soup for the Soul

This latest batch of wisdom, love and inspiration will warm your hearts and nourish your souls, whether you're "tasting" *Chicken Soup* for the first time, or have dipped your "spoon" many times before.

In the tradition of all the books in the original *Chicken Soup* series, this volume focuses on love; parents and parenting; teaching and learning; death and dying; perspective; overcoming obstacles; and eclectic wisdom. Contributors to *A 6th Bowl of Chicken Soup for the Soul* include: Erma Bombeck, Edgar Guest, Jay Leno, Rachel Naomi Remen, Robert A. Schuller, Dr. James Dobson, Dolly Parton and Cathy Rigby.

Code #6625 • $12.95

HCI's Spring Spirituality Series

"Let go of all things and allow yourself to become true and clean. We now have the opportunity to change our attitude and perceptions. Time is calling us, the world is calling us and, if you listen, your own inner voice is calling you."

—Dadi Janki

In this inspiring collection, framed by the stunning color images of French artist Marie Binder, Dadi Janki will guide you on an awakening spiritual journey. Chapters on Humility and Empowerment, Living the Vision, God, The World, Meditation, The Art of Living and Angels, will provide you with the tools to remove mental and emotional obstacles to self-fulfillment. Dadi Janki shows how every one of us can find our spiritual identity and make a very practical contribution to a better life and a better world.

Code # 6722 Paperback • $10.95

HCI's Spring Spirituality Series

Code #6781 • $7.95

The Man Who Couldn't See Himself

Whimsically illustrated, this is story of a man who has lost sight of who he is. Filled with loneliness he buys himself a dog, but before long, they are both lonely. Thus begins a sublime journey of a man to rediscover himself. In time and almost imperceptibly he realizes a shift in consciousness and becomes open to the mystery of love.

Ignite Your Intuition

Extraordinist Craig Karges is known to millions of television viewers for his remarkable demonstrations of extraordinary phenomena on *The Tonight Show with Jay Leno, Larry King Live*, and many other TV shows. In his new book, Karges reveals how to unlock the power within your own intuition—what he calls your natural psychic abilities. Be awakened to the possibility of realizing your own potential.

Code # 6765 • $10.95

Visionary Fiction from HCI

Code #6692 • $12.95

Wings of Destiny

Catherine Lanigan, best-selling author of *Romancing the Stone* and *Jewel of the Nile*, returns with a sweeping tale centered on the courage and irrepressible spirit of its protagonist heroine. The story of Jefferson Duke, who sacrifices the most precious of life's gifts: his heart and his granddaughter Barbara, who must betray him and, ultimately, learn the truth about herself and her own secret past.

Rings of Truth

A profound tale of a man's journey to discover his true self. Matt, a motivational speaker, has it all, until a spiritual apparition allows him to see that his material success means nothing if his soul is empty. Follow him on his transformative journey of awareness and awakening as he develops a greater understanding of who he his and teaches those around him, one truth at a time.
Code #7249 • $12.95

More from the *Chicken Soup for the Soul*® Series

#6161—$12.95

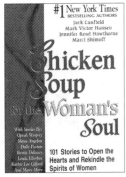

#4150—$12.95

#6218—$12.95

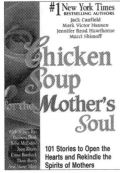

#4606—$12.95

Chicken Soup for the Soul® Series

Each one of these inspiring *New York Times* bestsellers brings you exceptional stories, tales and verses guaranteed to lift your spirits, soothe your soul and warm your heart! A perfect gift for anyone you love, including yourself!

A 5th Portion of Chicken Soup for the Soul, #5432—$12.95
A 4th Course of Chicken Soup for the Soul, #4592—$12.95
A 3rd Serving of Chicken Soup for the Soul, #3790—$12.95
A 2nd Helping of Chicken Soup for the Soul, #3316—$12.95
Chicken Soup for the Soul, #262X—$12.95

Selected books are also available in hardcover, large print, audiocassette and compact disc.

Available in bookstores everywhere or call 1-800-441-5569 for Visa or MasterCard orders. Prices do not include shipping and handling. Your response code is BKS. Order online at *http://www.hci-online.com*.